The Mystery of
Consciousness

The Mystery of Consciousness

John R. Searle

including exchanges with
Daniel C. Dennett
and
David J. Chalmers

A **New York Review** Book

New York

Published in the United States and Canada by:
The New York Review of Books
435 Hudson Street
New York, NY 10014

Most of the material in this book was first published in
The New York Review of Books in somewhat different form.

Library of Congress Cataloging-in-Publication Data

Searle, John R.
    The mystery of consciousness / John R. Searle and exchanges with
    Daniel C. Dennett and David Chalmers.
            p.   cm.
    Includes bibliographical references and index.
    ISBN 0-940322-06-4 (pbk.: alk. paper)
    1. Consciousness.   2. Mind and body.   I. Dennett, Daniel Clement.
    II. Chalmers, David John, 1966–   III. Title.
    B808.9.S43   1997
    128'.2—dc21   97-26044
                                                                CIP

ISBN 978-0-940322-06-6

Eleventh printing
Printed in the United States of America on acid-free paper

For Dagmar

Contents

Preface

This era is at once the most exciting and the most frustrating for the study of consciousness in my intellectual lifetime: exciting because consciousness has again become respectable, indeed almost central, as a subject of investigation in philosophy, psychology, cognitive science, and even neuroscience; frustrating because the whole subject is still plagued with mistakes and errors I thought had been long exposed.

This excitement—and some of the mistakes—are exemplified by the works discussed in this book, which is based on a series of articles that I published in *The New York Review of Books* between 1995 and 1997. The intervening time, and the larger scope of a book, have allowed me to expand and revise some of the original essays and to try to unify the entire discussion.

As I look over this material from the vantage point of the debates that have gone on—and still go on—about the issues discussed in these chapters, it seems to me that the greatest single philosophical obstacle to getting a satisfactory account of consciousness is our continued acceptance of a set of obsolete categories, and an accompanying set of presuppositions that we have inherited from our religious and philosophical tradition. We start off with the mistaken assumption that the notions of "mental" and "physical," of "dualism" and "monism," of "materialism" and "idealism" are clear and respectable notions as they stand, and that the issues have to be posed and resolved in these traditional terms. We also suppose that the notion of scientific reduction—by which complex phenomena can be explained by, and in some cases eliminated in favor of, the basic mechanisms that make them work—is clear and presents few difficulties. We then notice that consciousness, our ordinary states of sentience and awareness when we are awake, as well as our states of dreaming when we are asleep, seem very peculiar when we compare them with such "physical" phenomena as molecules or mountains. Compared to mountains and molecules, consciousness seems "mysterious," "ethereal," even "mystical." Consciousness does not seem to be "physical" in the way that other features of the brain, such as neuron firings, are physical. Nor does it seem to be reducible to physical processes by the usual sorts of scientific analyses that have worked for such physical properties as heat and solidity.

Many philosophers believe that if you grant real existence to consciousness you will be forced to some version of "dualism," the view that there are two metaphysically different kinds of phenomena in the universe, the mental and the physical. Indeed for many authors, the very definition of dualism implies that if you accept, in addition to such "physical" phenomena as mountains, "mental" phenomena such as pains, you are a dualist. But dualism as traditionally conceived seems a hopeless theory because, having made a strict distinction between the mental and the physical, it cannot then make the relation of the two intelligible. It seems that to accept dualism is to give up the entire scientific worldview that we have spent nearly four centuries to attain. So, what are we to do?

Many authors bite the bullet and accept dualism, for example, the physicist Roger Penrose and the philosopher David J. Chalmers, both discussed in the pages that follow. But in contemporary philosophy the most common move is to insist that materialism must be right and that we must eliminate consciousness by reducing it to something else. Daniel C. Dennett is an obvious example of a philosopher who adopts this position. Favorite candidates for the phenomena to which consciousness must be reduced are brain states described in purely "physical" terms and computer programs. But, as I argue in the book, all of these reductionist attempts to eliminate consciousness are as hopeless as the dualism they were designed to supplant. In a way they are worse, because they deny the real existence of the conscious states they were supposed to explain. They end up by denying the obvious fact that we all have inner, qualitative, subjective states such as our pains and joys, memories and perceptions, thoughts and feelings, moods, regrets, and hungers.

I believe the urge to reductionism and materialism derives from the underlying mistake of supposing that if we accept consciousness as having its own real existence, we will somehow be accepting dualism and rejecting the scientific worldview. If there is one theme that runs throughout this book it is this: consciousness is a natural, biological phenomenon. It is as much a part of our biological life as digestion, growth, or photosynthesis.

We are blinded to the natural, biological character of consciousness and other mental phenomena by our philosophical tradition, which makes "mental" and "physical" into two mutually exclusive categories. The way out is to reject both dualism and materialism, and accept that consciousness is both a qualitative, subjective "mental" phenomenon, and at the same time a natural part of the "physical" world. Conscious states are qualitative in the sense that for any conscious state, such as feeling a pain or worrying about the economic situation, there is something that it qualitatively feels like to be in that state, and they are subjective in the sense that they only exist when experienced by some human or other sort of "subject." Consciousness is a natural biological phenomenon that does not fit comfortably into either of the traditional categories of mental and physical. It is caused by lower-level microprocesses in the brain and it is a feature of the brain at the higher macro levels. To accept this "biological naturalism," as I like to call it, we first have to abandon the traditional categories.

Future generations, I suspect, will wonder why it took us so long in the twentieth century to see the centrality of consciousness in the understanding of our very existence as human beings. Why, for so long, did we think that consciousness did not matter, that it was unimportant? The paradox is that consciousness is the condition that makes it possible for anything at all to matter to anybody. Only to conscious agents can there ever be a question of anything mattering or having any importance at all.

My aim in writing this book is to appraise some of the significant and influential views on the problem of consciousness, and in so doing to present and try to justify my own views. I do not say that the books chosen for review here are the "best" books on the subject. On the contrary my opinions as to their different degrees of quality will emerge all too clearly in the following chapters. In my view the books range in quality from superb to dreadful. They were chosen for various reasons: some are excellent; others are influential, exemplary, suggestive, or symptomatic of current confusions. None of them solves the problem of consciousness, but some point the way toward a solution. We will understand consciousness when we understand in biological detail how the brain does it. How exactly does the brain cause our conscious states and processes, and how exactly do these states and processes function in our brains and in our lives generally?

I present my own views in the first and last chapters. Each of the other chapters is devoted to one of the other writers. Three of the chapters contain appendixes, chapter 4 because I wanted to separate some fairly technical material from the body of the chapter; and chapters 5 and 6 because two of the authors responded to the reviews of their books, and their responses together with my rejoinders are reprinted here as appendixes to the respective chapters.

I am indebted to a large number of people for help and advice in writing this book. First, and perhaps most important, five of the six authors under review, Francis Crick, Gerald Edelman, Penrose, Dennett, and Chalmers, have responded in various ways to my comments. I am especially grateful to Chalmers and Penrose for pointing out ways in which they think I have misunderstood their views in earlier versions of this material. Dennett's and Chalmers's published responses to my original reviews as well as my rejoinders are here in full in their original form.

Various colleagues read portions of the material and made helpful comments. I am especially grateful to Ned Block. I was helped enormously in understanding Gödel's theorem and Penrose's use of it by several mathematical logicians, especially Mack Stanley and William Craig. Robert Silvers of *The New York Review* is the best editor I have ever encountered, and I have benefited enormously from his relentless and implacable insistence on clear explanation. The great lesson I have learned from him is that it is possible to present difficult issues to non-specialists without sacrificing intellectual complexity. Special thanks are also due to my research assistant, Jennifer Hudin, and most of all to my wife, Dagmar Searle, to whom this book is dedicated.

Chapter One

Consciousness as a
Biological Problem

The most important problem in the biological sciences is one that until quite recently many scientists did not regard as a suitable subject for scientific investigation at all. It is this: How exactly do neurobiological processes in the brain cause consciousness? The enormous variety of stimuli that affect us—for example, when we taste wine, look at the sky, smell a rose, listen to a concert—trigger sequences of neurobiological processes that eventually cause unified, well-ordered, coherent, inner, subjective states of awareness or sentience. Now what exactly happens between the assault of the stimuli on our receptors and the experience of consciousness, and how exactly do the intermediate processes cause the conscious states? The problem, moreover, is not just about the perceptual cases I have mentioned, but includes the experiences of voluntary actions, as well as such inner processes as worrying about income taxes or trying to remember your mother-in-law's phone number. It is an amazing fact that everything in our conscious life, from feeling pains, tickles, and itches to—pick your favorite—

feeling the angst of postindustrial man under late capitalism or experiencing the ecstasy of skiing in deep powder, is caused by brain processes. As far as we know the relevant processes take place at the microlevels of synapses, neurons, neuron columns, and cell assemblies. All of our conscious life is caused by these lower-level processes, but we have only the foggiest idea of how it all works.

Well, you might ask, why don't the relevant specialists get on with it and figure out how it works? Why should it be any harder than finding out the causes of cancer? But there are a number of special features that make the problems raised by brain sciences even harder to solve. Some of the difficulties are practical: by current estimate, the human brain has over 100 billion neurons, and each neuron has synaptic connections with other neurons ranging in number from a few hundred to many tens of thousands. All of this enormously complex structure is massed together in a space smaller than a soccer ball. Furthermore, it is hard to work on the microelements in the brain without damaging them or killing the organism. In addition to the practical difficulties, there are several philosophical and theoretical obstacles and confusions that make it hard to pose and answer the right questions. For example, the common-sense way in which I have just posed the question, "How do brain processes cause consciousness?" is already philosophically loaded. Many philosophers and even some scientists think that the relation cannot be causal, because a causal relation between brain and consciousness seems to them to imply some version of dualism of brain and consciousness, which they want to reject on other grounds.

From the time of the ancient Greeks up to the latest

computational models of cognition, the entire subject of consciousness, and of its relation to the brain, has been something of a mess, and at least some of the mistakes in the history of the subject are repeated in recent examinations of the subject I will discuss here. Before discussing the latest work, I want to set the stage by clarifying some of the issues and correcting some of what seem to me the worst historical mistakes.

One issue can be dealt with swiftly. There is a problem that is supposed to be difficult but does not seem very serious to me, and that is the problem of defining "consciousness." It is supposed to be frightfully difficult to define the term. But if we distinguish between analytic definitions, which aim to analyze the underlying essence of a phenomenon, and common-sense definitions, which just identify what we are talking about, it does not seem to me at all difficult to give a commonsense definition of the term: "consciousness" refers to those states of sentience and awareness that typically begin when we awake from a dreamless sleep and continue until we go to sleep again, or fall into a coma or die or otherwise become "unconscious." Dreams are a form of consciousness, though of course quite different from full waking states. Consciousness so defined switches off and on. By this definition a system is either conscious or it isn't, but within the field of consciousness there are states of intensity ranging from drowsiness to full awareness. Consciousness so defined is an inner, first-person, qualitative phenomenon. Humans and higher animals are obviously conscious, but we do not know how far down the phylogenetic scale consciousness extends. Are fleas conscious, for example? At the present state of neurobiological knowledge, it is probably not useful to worry about such questions. We do not know enough biology to know where the cutoff point is. Also, the general phenomenon of consciousness should not be confused with the special case of self-consciousness. Most conscious states, feeling a pain, for example, do not necessarily involve self-consciousness. In some special cases, one is conscious of oneself as being in that state of consciousness. When worrying about one's tendency to worry too much, for example, one may become conscious of oneself as an inveterate worrier, but consciousness as such does not necessarily imply self-consciousness or self-awareness.

The first serious problem derives from intellectual history. In the seventeenth century Descartes and Galileo made a sharp distinction between the physical reality described by science and the mental reality of the soul, which they considered to be outside the scope of scientific research. This dualism of conscious mind and unconscious matter was useful in the scientific research of the time, both because it helped to get the religious authorities off scientists' backs and because the physical world was mathematically treatable in a way that the mind did not seem to be. But this dualism has become an obstacle in the twentieth century, because it seems to place consciousness and other mental phenomena outside the ordinary physical world and thus outside the realm of natural science. In my view we have to abandon dualism and start with the assumption that consciousness is an ordinary biological phenomenon comparable with growth, digestion, or the secretion of bile. But many people working in the sciences remain dualists and do not believe we can give a causal account of consciousness that shows it to be part of ordinary biological reality. Perhaps the most famous of these is the Nobel laureate neurobiologist

Sir John Eccles, who believes that God attaches the soul to the unborn fetus at the age of about three weeks.

Of the scientists I discuss here, the mathematician Roger Penrose is a dualist in the sense that he does not think we live in one unified world but rather that there is a separate mental world that is "grounded" in the physical world. Actually, he thinks we live in three worlds: a physical world, a mental world, and a world of abstract objects such as numbers and other mathematical entities. I will say more about this later.

But even if we treat consciousness as a biological phenomenon and thus as part of the ordinary physical world, as I urge we should, there are still many other mistakes to avoid. One I just mentioned: if brain processes cause consciousness, then it seems to many people that there must be two different things, brain processes as causes and conscious states as effects, and this seems to imply dualism. This second mistake derives in part from a flawed conception of causation. In our official theories of causation we typically suppose that all causal relations must be between discrete events ordered sequentially in time. For example, the shooting caused the death of the victim.

Certainly, many cause-and-effect relations are like that, but by no means all. Look around you at the objects in your vicinity and think of the causal explanation of the fact that the table exerts pressure on the rug. This is explained by the force of gravity, but gravity is not an event. Or think of the solidity of the table. It is explained causally by the behavior of the molecules of which the table is composed. But the solidity of the table is not an extra event; it is just a feature of the table. Such examples of non-event causation give us appropriate models for understanding the relation between my present state of consciousness and the underlying neurobiological processes that cause it. Lower-level processes in the brain cause my present state of consciousness, but that state is not a separate entity from my brain; rather it is just a feature of my brain at the present time. By the way, this analysis—that brain processes cause consciousness but that consciousness is itself *a feature of* the brain—provides us with a solution to the traditional mind–body problem, a solution which avoids both dualism and materialism, at least as these are traditionally conceived.

A third difficulty in our present intellectual situation is that we don't have anything like a clear idea of how brain processes, which are publicly observable, objective phenomena, could cause anything as peculiar as inner, qualitative states of awareness or sentience, states which are in some sense "private" to the possessor of the state. My pain has a certain qualitative feel and is accessible to me in a way that it is not accessible to you. Now how *could* these private, subjective, qualitative phenomena be caused by ordinary physical processes such as electrochemical neuron firings at the synapses of neurons? There is a special qualitative feel to each type of conscious state, and we are not in agreement about how to fit these subjective feelings into our overall view of the world as consisting of objective reality. Such states and events are sometimes called "qualia," and the problem of accounting for them within our overall worldview is called the problem of qualia. Among the interesting differences in the accounts of consciousness given by the writers whose work I discuss are their various divergent ways of coming to terms—or sometimes failing to come to terms—with the problem of qualia. I myself am hesitant to use the word "qualia" and its singular, "quale," because they give the impression that there are two separate phenomena, consciousness and qualia. But of course, all conscious phenomena are qualitative, subjective experiences, and hence are qualia. There are not two types of phenomena, consciousness and qualia. There is just consciousness, which is a series of qualitative states.

A fourth difficulty is peculiar to our intellectual climate right now, and that is the urge to take the computer metaphor of the mind too literally. Many people still think that the brain is a digital computer and that the conscious mind is a computer program, though mercifully this view is much less widespread than it was a decade ago. Construed in this way, the mind is to the brain as software is to hardware. There are different versions of the computational theory of the mind. The strongest is the one I have just stated: the mind is just a computer program. There is nothing else there. This view I call Strong Artificial Intelligence (Strong AI, for short) to distinguish it from the view that the computer is a useful tool in doing simulations of the mind, as it is useful in doing simulations of just about anything we can describe precisely, such as weather patterns or the flow of money in the economy. This more cautious view I call Weak AI.

Strong AI can be refuted swiftly, and indeed I did so in *The New York Review of Books* and elsewhere over fifteen years ago.[1] A computer is by definition a device that manipulates formal symbols. These are usually described as 0s and 1s, though any old symbol will do just as well. The inventor of the modern

---

1. "The Myth of the Computer," *The New York Review of Books*, April 29, 1982, pp. 3–6; "Minds, Brains and Programs," *Behavioral and Brain Sciences*, Vol. 3 (1980), pp. 417–457.

conception of computation, Alan Turing, put this point by saying that a computing machine can be thought of as a device that contains a head that scans a tape. On the tape are printed 0s and 1s. The machine can perform exactly four operations. It can move the tape one square to the left, it can move it one square to the right, it can erase a 0 and print a 1, and it can erase a 1 and print a 0. It performs these operations according to a set of rules of the form "under condition C perform act A." These rules are called the program. Modern computers work by encoding information in the binary code of zeroes and ones, translating the encoded information into electrical impulses and then processing the information according to the rules of the program.

It is one of the most amazing intellectual achievements of the twentieth century that we have been able to do so much with such a limited mechanism, but for present purposes the important point is that the mechanism is defined entirely in terms of the manipulation of symbols. Computation, so defined, is a purely syntactical set of operations, in the sense that the only features of the symbols that matter for the implementation of the program are the formal or syntactical features. But we know from our own experience that the mind has something more going on in it than the manipulation of formal symbols; minds have contents. For example, when we are thinking in English, the English words going through our minds are not just uninterpreted formal symbols; rather, we know what they mean. For us the words have a meaning, or semantics. The mind could not be just a computer program, because the formal symbols of the computer program by themselves are not sufficient to guarantee the presence of the semantic content that occurs in actual minds.

I have illustrated this point with a simple thought experiment. Imagine that you carry out the steps in a program for answering questions in a language you do not understand. I do not understand Chinese, so I imagine that I am locked in a room with a lot of boxes of Chinese symbols (the database), I get small bunches of Chinese symbols passed to me (questions in Chinese), and I look up in a rule book (the program) what I am supposed to do. I perform certain operations on the symbols in accordance with the rules (that is, I carry out the steps in the program) and give back small bunches of symbols (answers to the questions) to those outside the room. I am the computer implementing a program for answering questions in Chinese, but all the same I do not understand a word of Chinese. And this is the point: *if I do not understand Chinese solely on the basis of implementing a computer program for understanding Chinese, then neither does any other digital computer solely on that basis, because no digital computer has anything I do not have.*

This is such a simple and decisive argument that I am embarrassed to have to repeat it, but in the years since I first published it there must have been over a hundred published attacks on it, including some in Daniel Dennett's *Consciousness Explained*, one of the books under discussion. The Chinese Room Argument—as it has come to be called—has a simple three-step structure:

1. Programs are entirely syntactical.
2. Minds have a semantics.
3. Syntax is not the same as, nor by itself sufficient for, semantics.

Therefore programs are not minds. Q.E.D.

I want these steps to be understood in the most obvious and natural way. Step 1 just articulates the essential feature of Turing's definitions: the program written down consists entirely in rules concerning syntactical entities, that is, rules for manipulating symbols. And the implemented program, the program actually running, consists entirely in those very syntactical manipulations. The physics of the implementing medium—that is, the actual physical-electrical-chemical properties of the computer in front of me—is irrelevant to computation. The only physical requirement is that the machine must be rich enough and stable enough to carry out the steps in the program. Currently we happen to use silicon chips for this purpose, but there is no essential connection whatever between the physics and chemistry of silicon and the abstract formal properties of computer programs.

Step 2 just says what we all know about human thinking: when we think in words or other symbols we have to know what those words and symbols mean. That is why I can think in English but not in Chinese. My mind has more than uninterpreted formal symbols running through it; it has mental contents or semantic contents.

Step 3 states the general principle that the Chinese Room thought experiment illustrates: merely manipulating formal symbols is not in and of itself constitutive of having semantic contents, nor is it sufficient by itself to guarantee the presence of semantic contents. It does not matter how well the system can imitate the behavior of someone who really does understand, nor how complex the symbol manipulations are; you cannot milk semantics out of syntactical processes alone.

In order to refute the argument you would have to show that one of those premises is false, and that is not a likely prospect.

Many letters to *The New York Review of Books* revealed misunderstandings of the argument. Several people thought I was trying to prove that "machines can't think" or even that "computers can't think." Both of these are misunderstandings. The brain is a machine, a biological machine, and it can think. Therefore at least some machines can think, and for all we know it might be possible to build artificial brains that can also think. Furthermore, human brains sometimes compute. They add 2 + 2 and get 4, for example. So, on one definition of a computer, brains are computers because they compute. Therefore some computers can think—your brain and mine, for example.

Another misunderstanding is to suppose that I am denying that a given physical computer might have consciousness as an "emergent property." After all, if brains can have consciousness as an emergent property, why not other sorts of machinery? But Strong AI is not about the specific capacities of computer hardware to produce emergent properties. Any given commercial computer has all sorts of emergent properties. My computer gives off heat, it makes a humming sound, and with certain programs it makes certain buzzing and crunching noises. All of this is totally irrelevant to Strong AI. Strong AI does not claim that certain sorts of hardware might give off mental states the way they give off heat or that the properties of the hardware might cause the system to have mental states. Rather, Strong AI claims that implementing the right program in *any hardware at all* is constitutive of mental states. To repeat: the thesis of Strong AI is not that a computer might "give off" or have mental states as emergent properties, but rather that *the implemented program, by itself, is constitutive of having a mind. The implemented program, by itself, guarantees mental life.* And it is this thesis that the Chinese Room Argument refutes. The refutation reminds us that the program is *defined* purely syntactically, and that syntax by itself is not enough to guarantee the presence of mental, semantic content.

I offer no a priori proof that this physical computer is not conscious any more than I offer a proof that this chair is not conscious. Biologically speaking, I think the idea that they might be conscious is simply out of the question. But in any case it is irrelevant to Strong AI, which is about programs and not about the emergent properties of silicon or other physical substances.

It now seems to me that the Chinese Room Argument, if anything, concedes too much to Strong AI in that it concedes that the theory is at least false. I now think it is incoherent, and here is why. Ask yourself what fact about the machine I am now writing this on makes its operations syntactical or symbolic. As far as its physics is concerned it is just a very complex electronic circuit. The fact that makes these electrical pulses symbolic is the same sort of fact that makes the ink marks on the pages of a book into symbols: we have designed, programmed, printed, and manufactured these systems so we can treat and use these things as symbols. Syntax, in short, is not intrinsic to the physics of the system but is in the eye of the beholder. Except for the few cases of conscious agents actually going through a computation, adding 2 + 2 to get 4, for example, computation is not an intrinsic process in nature like digestion or photosynthesis, but exists only relative to some agent who gives a computational interpretation to the physics. The upshot is that computation is not intrinsic to nature but is relative to the observer or user.

This is an important point so I will repeat it. The natural sciences typically deal with those features of nature that are intrinsic or observer-independent in the sense that their existence does not depend on what anybody thinks. Examples of such features are mass, photosynthesis, electric charge, and mitosis. The social sciences often deal with features that are observer-dependent or observer-relative in the sense that their existence depends on how humans treat them, use them, or otherwise think of them. Examples of such features are money, property, and marriage. A bit of paper, for example, is only money relative to the fact that people think that it is money. The fact that this object consists of cellulose fibers is observer-independent; the fact that it is a twenty-dollar bill is observer-relative. As you read the sheet of paper in front of you, you see certain ink marks. The chemical composition of the ink marks is intrinsic, but the fact that they are English words, sentences, or other sorts of symbols is observer-relative. My present state of consciousness is intrinsic in this sense: I am conscious regardless of what anybody else thinks.

Now, how is it with computation? Is it observer-independent or observer-relative? Well, there are a certain limited number of cases where conscious human beings actually consciously compute, in the old-fashioned sense of the word that, for example, they compute the sum of 2 + 2 and get 4. Such cases are clearly observer-independent in the sense that no outside observer has to treat them or think of them as computing in order for them to be actually computing. But what about commercial computers? What about the machine in front of me, for example? What fact of physics and chemistry makes these electrical pulses into computational symbols? No fact whatever. The words "symbol," "syntax," and "computation" do not name intrinsic features of nature like "tectonic plate," "electron," or "consciousness." The electrical impulses are observer-independent; but the computational interpretation is relative to observers, users, programmers, etc. To say that the computational interpretation is observer-relative does not imply that it is arbitrary or capricious. A great deal of effort and money is spent to design and produce electric machinery that can carry out the desired kind of computational interpretation.

The consequence for our present discussion is that the question "Is the brain a digital computer?" lacks a clear sense. If it asks, "Is the brain intrinsically a digital computer?" the answer is trivially no, because apart from mental thought processes, nothing is intrinsically a digital computer; something is a computer only relative to the assignment of a computational interpretation. If it asks, "Can you assign a computational interpretation to the brain?" the answer is trivially yes, because you can assign a computational interpretation to anything. For example, the window in front of me is a very simple computer. Window open = 1, window closed = 0. That is, if we accept Turing's definition according to which anything to which you can assign a 0 and a 1 is a computer, then the window is a simple and trivial computer. You could never discover computational processes in nature independently of human interpretation because any physical process you might find is computational only relative to some interpretation. This is an obvious point and I should have seen it long ago.

The upshot is that Strong AI, which prides itself on its "materialism" and on the view that the brain is a machine, is not nearly materialistic enough. The brain is indeed a machine, an organic machine; and its processes, such as neuron firings, are organic machine processes. But computation is not a machine process like neuron firing or internal combustion; rather, computation is an abstract mathematical process that exists only relative to conscious observers and interpreters. Observers such as ourselves have found ways to implement computation on silicon-based electrical machines, but that does not make computation into something electrical or chemical.

This is a different argument from the Chinese Room Argument, but it is deeper. The Chinese Room Argument showed that semantics is not intrinsic to syntax; this shows that syntax is not intrinsic to physics.

I reject Strong AI but accept Weak AI. Of the authors I will discuss here, Dennett and David Chalmers each hold a version of Strong AI and Roger Penrose rejects even Weak AI. He thinks the mind cannot even be simulated on a computer. The neurobiologist Gerald Edelman accepts the Chinese Room Argument against Strong AI and presents some other arguments of his own, but he accepts Weak AI; indeed, he makes powerful use of computer models in his research on the brain, as we will see.

To summarize my general position, then, on how brain research can proceed in answering the questions that bother us: the brain is an organ like any other; it is an organic machine. Consciousness is caused by lower-level neuronal processes in the brain and is itself a feature of the brain.

Because it is a feature that emerges from certain neuronal activities, we can think of it as an "emergent property" of the brain. An emergent property of a system is one that is causally explained by the behavior of the elements of the system; but it is not a property of any individual elements and it cannot be explained simply as a summation of the properties of those elements. The liquidity of water is a good example: the behavior of the H_2O molecules explains liquidity but the individual molecules are not liquid.

Computers play the same role in studying the brain that they play in any other discipline. They are immensely useful devices for simulating brain processes. But the simulation of mental states is no more a mental state than the simulation of an explosion is itself an explosion.

Chapter Two

Francis Crick, the Binding Problem, and the Hypothesis of Forty Hertz

Until recently there was a reluctance among scientists to tackle the problem of consciousness. Now all that has changed, and there has been a spate of books on the subject by biologists, mathematicians, and physicists as well as philosophers. Of the scientists I will consider, Francis Crick attempts to give the simplest and most direct account of what we know about how the brain works in his *The Astonishing Hypothesis: The Scientific Search for the Soul.*[1] The astonishing hypothesis on which the book is based is

> that "You," your joys and your sorrows, your memories and your ambitions, your sense of personal identity and free will, are in fact no more than the behavior of a vast assembly of nerve cells and their associated molecules. [p. 3]

---

1. Simon and Schuster, 1994.

I have seen reviews of Crick's book which complained that it is not at all astonishing in this day and age to be told that what goes on in our skulls is responsible for the whole of our mental life, and that anyone with a modicum of scientific education will accept Crick's hypothesis as something of a platitude. I do not think this is a fair complaint. There are two parts to Crick's astonishment. The first is that all of our mental life has a material existence in the brain—and that is indeed not very astonishing—but the second is that, more interestingly, the specific mechanisms in the brain that are responsible for our mental life are neurons and their associated molecules, such as neurotransmitter molecules. I, for one, am always amazed by the specificity of biological systems, and, in the case of the brain, the specificity takes a form you could not have predicted just from knowing what it does. If you were designing an organic machine to pump blood you might come up with something like a heart, but if you were designing a machine to produce consciousness, who would think of a hundred billion neurons?

Crick is not clear about distinguishing causal explanations of consciousness from reductionist eliminations of consciousness. The passage I quoted above makes it look as if he is denying that we have conscious experiences in addition to having neuron firings. But I think that a careful reading of the book shows that what he means is something like the claim that I advanced earlier: all of our conscious experiences are *explained by* the behavior of neurons and are themselves *emergent properties* of the system of neurons.

The fact that the explanatory part of Crick's claim is standard neurobiological orthodoxy today, and will astonish few of the people who are likely to read the book, should not prevent us from agreeing that it is amazing how the brain does so much with such a limited mechanism. Furthermore, not everyone who works in this field agrees that the neuron is the essential functional element. Penrose believes neurons are already too big, and he wants to account for consciousness at a level of much smaller quantum mechanical phenomena. Edelman thinks neurons are too small for most functions and regards the functional elements as "neuronal groups."

Crick takes visual perception as his wedge for trying to break into the problem of consciousness. I think this is a good choice if only because so much work in the brain sciences has already been done on the anatomy and physiology of seeing. But one problem with it is that the operation of the visual system is astonishingly complicated. The simple act of recognizing a friend's face in a crowd requires far more by way of processing than we are able to understand at present. My guess —and it is just a guess—is that when we finally break through to understanding how neuron firings cause consciousness or sentience, it is likely to come from understanding a simpler system in the human brain. However, this does not detract from the interest, indeed fascination, with which we are led by Crick through the layers of cells in the retina to the lateral geniculate nucleus and back to the visual cortex and then through the different areas of the cortex.

We do not really know how it all works in detail, but here is a broad outline (fig. 1): light waves reflected off objects attack the photoreceptor cells in the retina of the eyeball. These cells are the famous rods and cones, and they form the first of five layers of retinal cells through which the signal

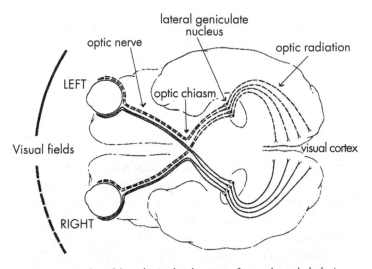

Fig. 1. An outline of the early visual pathways seen from underneath the brain. Notice that the right visual field influences the left side of the brain, and vice versa. The connections related to the right visual field are shown by lines of dashes

passes. The others are called the horizontal, bipolar, amacrine, and ganglion cells. The ganglion cells more or less ooze into the optic nerve, and the signal goes along the optic nerve over the optic chiasm to a portion in the middle of the brain called the lateral geniculate nucleus (LGN). The LGN acts as a kind of relay station, sending the signals to the visual cortex which is at the back of your skull. We used to think, when I first got interested in these questions, that there were three portions to the visual cortex, zones 17, 18, and 19, so labeled by K. Brodmann in the early part of this century when he made his famous map of the brain. Now we think this is much too crude. We have now counted up to seven visual areas, called V1, V2, etc., and we are still counting. Anyhow, the signal goes

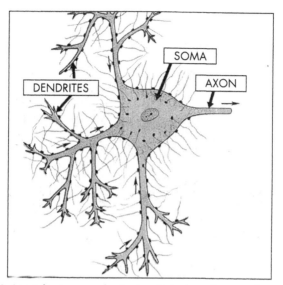

Fig. 2. A typical motoneuron, showing synaptic knobs on the neuronal soma and dendrites. Note also the single axon

through the various visual areas and there is a good deal of feedback to the LGN. Eventually the whole process causes a conscious visual experience, and how exactly that happens is what we are trying to figure out.

How does the neuron work? A neuron is a cell like any other, with a cell membrane and a central nucleus (fig. 2). Neurons differ however in certain remarkable ways, both anatomically and physiologically, from other sorts of cells. There are many different types of neuron, but the typical, garden-variety neuron has a longish, threadlike protuberance called an axon growing out of one side and a bunch of spiny, somewhat shorter, spiky threads with branches called dendrites on the other side. Each neuron receives signals through

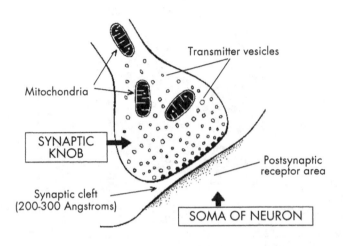

Fig. 3. Physiologic anatomy of the synapse

its dendrites, processes them in its cell body, or soma, and
then fires a signal through its axon to the next neurons in line.
The neuron fires by sending an electrical impulse down the
axon. The axon of one neuron, however, is not directly con-
nected to the dendrites of other neurons, but rather the point
at which the signal is transmitted from one cell to the next is
a small gap called a synaptic cleft (fig. 3). A synapse typically
consists of a bump on the axon, called a "bouton," or "synaptic
knob," which sticks out in roughly the shape of a mushroom,
and typically fits next to a spinelike protrusion on the surface
of the dendrite. The area between the bouton and the postsynaptic dendritic surface is the synaptic cleft, and when the
neuron fires the signal is transmitted across it.

The signal is transmitted not by a direct electrical connection between bouton and dendritic surface but by the release of small amounts of fluids called neurotransmitters. When the electrical signal travels from the cell body down the axon to the end of a bouton, it causes the release of neurotransmitter fluids into the synaptic cleft. These make contact with receptors on the postsynaptic dendritic side. This causes gates to open, and ions—electrically charged atoms and groups of atoms—flow in or out of the dendritic side, thus altering the electrical charge of the dendrite. The pattern then is this: there is an electrical signal on the axon side, followed by chemical transmission in the synaptic cleft, followed by an electrical signal on the dendrite side. The cell gets a whole bunch of signals from its dendrites, it does a summation of them in its cell body, and on the basis of the summation it adjusts its rate of firing to the next cells in line.

Neurons receive both excitatory signals, that is, signals which tend to increase their rate of firing, and inhibitory signals, signals which tend to decrease their rate of firing. Oddly enough, though each neuron receives both excitatory and inhibitory signals, each neuron sends out only one or the other type of signal. As far as we know, with few exceptions, a neuron is either an excitatory or an inhibitory neuron.

Now what is astonishing is this: as far as our mental life is concerned, that story I just told you about neurons is the entire causal basis of our conscious life. I left out various details about ion channels, receptors, and different types of neurotransmitters, but our entire mental life is caused by the behavior of neurons and all they do is increase or decrease their rates of firing. When, for example, we store memories, it seems we must store them somehow in the synaptic connections between neurons.

Crick is remarkably good not only at summarizing the simple account of brain functioning but at trying to integrate it with work in many related fields, including psychology, cognitive science, and the use of computers for neuronal net modeling, among others.

Crick is generally hostile to philosophers and philosophy, but the price of having contempt for philosophy is that you make philosophical mistakes. Most of these do not seriously damage his main argument, but they are annoying and unnecessary. I will mention three philosophical errors that I think are really serious.

First, he misunderstands the problem of qualia. He thinks it is primarily a problem about the way one person has knowledge of another person's qualia. "The problem springs from the fact that the redness of red that I perceive so vividly cannot be precisely communicated to another human being" (p. 9). But that is not the problem, or rather it is only one small part of the problem. Even for a system of whose qualia I have near-perfect knowledge, myself for example, the problem of qualia is serious. It is this: How is it possible for physical, objective, quantitatively describable neuron firings to cause qualitative, private, subjective experiences? How, to put it naively, does the brain get us over the hump from electrochemistry to feeling? That is the hard part of the mind–body problem that is left over after we see that consciousness must be caused by brain processes and is itself a feature of the brain.

Furthermore, the problem of qualia is not just an aspect of the problem of consciousness; it *is* the problem of consciousness. You can talk about various other features of consciousness—for example, the powers that the visual system has to discriminate colors—but to the extent that you are talking about conscious discrimination you are talking about qualia. I think that the term "qualia" is misleading because it suggests that the quale of a state of consciousness might be carved off from the rest of the consciousness and set on one side, as if you could talk about the rest of the problem of consciousness while ignoring the subjective, qualitative feel of consciousness. But you can't set qualia on one side, because if you do there is no consciousness left over.

Second, Crick is inconsistent in his account of the reduction of consciousness to neuron firings. He talks reductionist talk, but the account he gives is not at all reductionist in nature. Or rather there are at least two senses of "reduction" that he fails to distinguish. In one sense, reduction is eliminative. We get rid of the reduced phenomenon by showing that it is really something else. Sunsets are a good example. The sun does not really set over Mount Tamalpais; rather, the appearance of the setting sun is an illusion entirely explained by the rotation of the earth on its axis relative to the sun. But in another sense of reduction we explain a phenomenon but do not get rid of it. Thus the solidity of an object is entirely explained by the behavior of molecules, but this does not show that no object is really solid or that there is no distinction between, say, solidity and liquidity. Now Crick talks as if he wants an eliminative reduction of consciousness, but in fact the direction in his book is toward a causal explanation. He does not attempt to show that consciousness does not really exist. He gives the game away when he says, entirely correctly in my view, that consciousness is an emergent property of the brain. Complex sensations, he says, are emergent properties that "arise in the brain from the interactions of its many parts" (p. 11).

The puzzle is that Crick preaches eliminative reductionism while he practices causal emergentism. The standard argument in philosophy against an eliminative reduction of consciousness is that even if we had a perfect science of neurobiology there would still be two distinct features, the neurobiological pattern of neuron firings and the feeling of pain, for example. The neuron firings cause the feeling, but they are not the same thing as the feeling. In different versions this argument is advanced by, among other philosophers, Thomas Nagel, Saul Kripke, Frank Jackson, and myself. Crick mistakenly endorses an argument against this anti-reductionism, one made by Paul and Patricia Churchland. Their argument is a bad argument and I might as well say why I think so. They think the standard philosophical account is based on the following obviously flawed argument:

1. Sam knows his feeling is a pain.

2. Sam does not know that his feeling is a pattern of neuron firings.

3. Therefore Sam's feeling is not a pattern of neuron firings.[2]

---

2. They have advanced this argument in a number of places, most recently in Paul Churchland's *The Engine of Reason, the Seat of the Soul* (MIT Press, 1995), pp. 195–208.

The Churchlands point out that this argument is fallacious, but they are mistaken in thinking that it is the argument used by their opponents. The argument they are attacking is "epistemic"; it is about knowledge. But the argument for
the irreducibility of consciousness is not epistemic; it is about
how things are in the world. It is about ontology. There are
different ways of spelling it out but the fundamental point of
each is the same: the sheer qualitative feel of pain is a very different feature of the brain from the pattern of neuron firings
that cause the pain. So you can get a causal reduction of pain
to neuron firings but not an ontological reduction. That is,
you can give a complete causal account of why we feel pain,
but that does not show that pains do not really exist.

Third, Crick is unclear about the logical structure of the
explanation he is offering, and even on the most sympathetic
reading it seems to be inconsistent. I have so far been interpreting him as seeking a causal explanation of visual consciousness, and his talk of "mechanism" and "explanation"
supports that interpretation. But he never says clearly that he
is offering a causal explanation of how brain processes produce
visual awareness. His preferred way of speaking is to say that
he is looking for the "neural correlates" of consciousness (e.g.,
p. 9 and pp. 204–207). But on his own terms "neural correlates" cannot be the right expression. First, a correlation is a
relation between two different things, but a relation between
two things is inconsistent with the eliminative reductionist
line that Crick thinks he is espousing. On the eliminative
reductionist view there should be only one thing, neuron firings. Second, and more important, even if we strip away the
reductionist mistake, correlations by themselves would not

explain anything. Think of the sight of lightning and the sound of thunder. The sight and sound are perfectly correlated, but without a causal theory, you do not have an explanation.

Furthermore, Crick is unclear about the relation between the visual experiences and the objects in the world that they are experiences of. Sometimes he says the visual experience is a "symbolic description" (p. 32) or "symbolic interpretation" of the world (p. 33). Sometimes he says the neuronal processes "represent" objects in the world (p. 206). He is even led to deny that we have direct perceptual awareness of objects in the world, and for that conclusion he uses a bad argument right out of seventeenth-century philosophy (p. 33). He says that since our interpretations can occasionally be wrong, we have no direct knowledge of objects in the world. This argument is in both Descartes and Hume, but it is a fallacy. From the fact that our perceptual experiences are always mediated by brain processes (how else could we have them?) and the fact that they are typically subject to illusions of various kinds, it does not follow that we never see the real world but only "symbolic descriptions" or "symbolic interpretations" of the world. In the standard case, such as when I look at my watch, I really see the real watch. I do not see a "description" or an "interpretation" of the watch.

I believe that Crick has been badly advised philosophically, but fortunately you can strip away the philosophical confusions and still find an excellent book. What I think in the end he wants, and what in any case I want, is a causal explanation of consciousness, whether visual or otherwise. Photons reflected off objects attack the photoreceptor cells of the retina and this sets up a series of neuronal processes (the retina being part of the brain), which eventually result, if all goes well, in a visual experience that is a perception of the very object that originally reflected the photons. That is the right way to think of it, as I hope he would agree.

What, then, is Crick's solution to the problem of consciousness? One of the most appealing features of Crick's book is his willingness, indeed eagerness, to admit how little we know. But given what we do know he makes some speculations. To explain his speculations about consciousness, I need to say something about what neurobiologists call the "binding problem." We know that the visual system has cells and indeed regions that are specially responsive to particular features of objects such as color, shape, movement, lines, angles, etc. But when we see an object we have a unified experience of a single object. How does the brain bind all of these different stimuli into a single unified experience of an object? The problem extends across the different modes of perception. All of my experiences at any given time are part of one big unified conscious experience. Thus, for example, right now I am thinking about visual consciousness, I am looking at a computer terminal, I can see my dog peripherally out of my left eye, I feel the weight of my body against the chair, I hear a stream outside my window, and all of these experiences, as well as others I could name, are parts of my one unified total conscious state at this moment. (Kant, with his usual gift for catchy phrases, called this the "transcendental unity of apperception.")

Crick says the binding problem is "the problem of how these neurons temporarily become active as a unit" (p. 208). But that is not the binding problem; rather, it is one possible approach to solving the binding problem. For example, a possible approach to solving the binding problem for vision has been proposed by various researchers, most importantly by Wolf Singer and his colleagues in Frankfurt.[3] They think that the solution might consist in the synchronization of firing of spatially separated neurons that are responsive to the different features of an object. Neurons responsive to shape, color, and movement, for example, fire in synchrony in the general range of forty firings per second (40 hertz). Crick and his colleague Christof Koch take this hypothesis a step further and suggest that maybe synchronized neuron firing in this range (roughly 40 hertz, but as low as 35 and as high as 75) might be the "brain correlate" of visual consciousness.

Furthermore, the thalamus appears to play a central role in consciousness, and consciousness in particular appears to depend on the circuits connecting the thalamus and the cortex, especially cortical layers four and six. So Crick speculates that perhaps synchronized firing in the range of 40 hertz in the networks connecting the thalamus and the cortex might be the key to solving the problem of consciousness.

I admire Crick's willingness to speculate, but the nature of the speculation reveals how far we have yet to go. Suppose it turned out that consciousness is invariably correlated with neuron firing rates of 40 hertz in neuronal circuits connecting the thalamus to the cortex. Would that be an explanation of

3. W. Singer, "Development and plasticity of cortical processing architectures," *Science* 270 (1995), pp. 758–764; W. Singer, "Synchronization of cortical activity and its putative role in information processing and learning," *Annual Review of Physiology* 55 (1993), pp. 349–375; W. Singer and C. M. Gray, "Visual feature integration and the temporal correlation hypothesis," *Annual Review of Neuroscience* 18 (1995), pp. 555–586.

consciousness? No. We would never accept it, as it stands, as an explanation. We would regard it as a tremendous step forward, but we would still want to know, how does it work? It would be like knowing that car movements are "correlated with" the oxidization of hydrocarbons under the hood. You still need to know the mechanisms by which the oxidization of hydrocarbons produces, i.e., *causes*, the movement of the wheels. Even if Crick's speculations turn out to be 100 percent correct we still need to know the mechanisms whereby the neural correlates cause the conscious feelings, and we are a long way from even knowing the form such an explanation might take.

Crick has written a good and useful book. He knows a lot, and he explains it clearly. Most of my objections are to his philosophical claims and presuppositions, but when you read the book you can ignore the philosophical parts and just learn about the psychology of vision and about brain science. The limitations of the neurobiological parts of the book are the limitations of the subject right now: we do not know how the psychology of vision and neurophysiology hang together, and we do not know how brain processes cause consciousness, whether visual consciousness or otherwise.

Chapter Three

Gerald Edelman and Reentry Mapping

Of the neurobiological theories of consciousness I have seen, the most impressively worked out and the most profound is that of Gerald Edelman. The two books I will discuss here are the third and the fourth in a series that began with *Neural Darwinism* and *Topobiology*. The aim of the series is to construct a global theory of the brain that situates brain science in relation to physics and evolutionary biology. The centerpiece of the series is the theory of consciousness advanced in *The Remembered Present* and summarized in *Bright Air, Brilliant Fire*.[1]

In order to explain Edelman's theory of consciousness I need first to explain briefly some of the central concepts and theories which he uses, especially those he uses to develop a theory of perceptual categorization. The best way to begin is

---

1. *Neural Darwinism: The Theory of Neuronal Group Selection* (BasicBooks, 1987); *Topobiology: An Introduction to Molecular Embryology* (BasicBooks, 1988); *The Remembered Present: A Biological Theory of Consciousness* (BasicBooks, 1989); and *Bright Air, Brilliant Fire: On the Matter of the Mind* (BasicBooks, 1992).

to compare Edelman's project to Crick's. As we saw in chapter 2, Crick wants to extend an account of the binding problem to a general account of consciousness. The "binding problem" poses the question of how different stimulus inputs to different parts of the brain are bound together so as to produce a single, unified experience, for example, of seeing a cat. Similarly, Edelman wants to extend an account of the development of perceptual categories—categories ranging from shapes, color, and movement to objects such as cats and dogs—into a general account of consciousness. In a word, Crick uses the binding problem for visual perception as the entering wedge to consciousness, while Edelman uses categorization as his entering wedge.

The first idea central to Edelman is the notion of maps. A map is a sheet of neurons in the brain where the points on the sheet are systematically related to the corresponding points on a sheet of receptor cells, such as the surface of the skin or the retina of the eye. Maps may also be related to other maps. In the human visual system there are over thirty maps in the visual cortex alone. It is important to emphasize that a map is supposed to be an actual piece of brain anatomy. We are talking about sheets of neurons. These sheets are identified as "maps" because the points on them have systematic relations to points on other sheets, and this is important for the phenomenon of reentry, as we will shortly see.

The second idea is his theory of Neuronal Group Selection. According to Edelman, we should not think of brain development, especially in matters such as perceptual categorization and memory, as a matter of the brain learning from the impact of the environment. Rather, the brain is genetically equipped from birth with an overabundance of neuronal groups and it develops by a mechanism which is like Darwinian natural selection: some neuronal groups die out, others survive and are strengthened. In some parts of the brain, as many as 70 percent of the neurons die before the brain reaches maturity. The unit which gets selected is not the individual neuron, but neuronal groups of hundreds to millions of cells. The basic point is that the brain is not an *instructional* mechanism, but a *selectional* mechanism; that is, the brain does not develop by alterations in a fixed set of neurons, but by selection processes that eliminate some neuronal groups and strengthen others.

The third, and the most important, idea is that of *reentry*. Reentry is a process by which parallel signals go back and forth between maps. Map A signals to map B and map B signals back. The signals enter B from A and then reenter back into A. Edelman is eager to insist that reentry is not just feedback, because there can be many parallel pathways operating simultaneously.

Now how is all this supposed to give rise to perceptual categories and generalizations? Edelman's prose is not very clear at this point, but the idea that emerges is this: the brain has a problem to solve. It has to develop perceptual categories beginning with shapes, color, movement, and eventually including objects—tree, horse, and cup—and it has to be able to abstract general concepts. It has to do all this in a situation where the world is not already labeled and divided up into categories, and in which the brain has no program in advance and no homunculus inside to guide it.

How does it solve the problem? It has a large number of stimulus inputs for any given category—some stimuli are from the borders or edges of an object, others from its color, etc.—and after many stimulus inputs, particular patterns of neuronal groups will be selected in maps. But now similar signals will activate the previously selected neuronal groups not only in one map but also in another map or even in a whole group of maps, because the operations in the different maps are linked together by the reentry channels. Each map can use discriminations made by other maps for its own operations. Thus one map might figure out the borders of an object, another might figure out its movements, and the reentry mechanisms might enable yet other maps to figure out the shape of the object from its borders and its movements (*The Remembered Present*, p. 72 ff.).

So the result is that you can get a unified representation of objects in the world even though the representation is distributed over many different areas of the brain. Different maps in different areas are busy signaling to each other through the reentry pathways. This leads to the possibility of categorization and simple generalization without needing a program or a homunculus. When you get maps all over the brain signaling to each other by reentry you have what Edelman calls "global mapping," and this allows the system not only to have perceptual categories and generalization but also to coordinate perception and action.

This is a working hypothesis and not an established theory. Edelman does not claim to have proven that this is how the brain works in forming perceptual categories. But the hypothesis is made at least plausible by the fact that Edelman's research group has designed Weak AI computer models of a robot ("Darwin III") that can acquire perceptual categories and can generalize them by using these mechanisms. The robot has a simulated "eye" and a "hand-arm" with which it flails about. It explores with these modalities and "decides" that something is an object, that it is striped, and that it is bumpy. It distinguishes objects which are both striped and bumpy from those that are striped or bumpy but not both (*Bright Air, Brilliant Fire*, pp. 91–93).[2]

It is important to emphasize that none of these processes so far is conscious. When Edelman talks about perceptual *categorization* he is not talking about conscious perceptual *experiences*. His strategy is to try to build up consciousness out of a series of processes, beginning with categorization, which are not supposed to be thought of as already conscious. It would beg the question to assume these are conscious from the start.

The question then is, how do we get from the apparatus I have described so far to conscious experiences? What more is needed? Edelman devotes most of the *The Remembered Present* to answering this question, and any brief summary is bound to be inadequate. It is essential to distinguish between "primary consciousness," which is a matter of having what he calls imagery, by which he means simple sensations and perceptual experiences, and "higher-order consciousness," which includes self-consciousness and language. Edelman's biggest problem is accounting for primary consciousness, because higher-order consciousness is built up out of processes that are already conscious, i.e., that have primary consciousness. In order to have

---

2. It is perhaps worth pointing out that Darwin III is not a physical robot that clonks around the room, but a picture of a robot, a simulation of a robot on a computer.

primary consciousness in addition to the mechanisms just described, the brain needs at least the following:

1. It must have memory. Memory for Edelman is not just a passive process of storing but an active process of recategorizing on the basis of previous categorizations. Edelman is not good at giving examples but what he seems to have in mind is this: suppose an animal has acquired a perceptual category of cats. It acquires this category through the experience of seeing a cat and organizing its experience by way of the reentrant maps. Then the next time it sees a cat, and thus has a similar perceptual input, it recategorizes the input by enhancing the previously established categorization. It does this by changes in the population of synapses in the global mapping. It does not just *recall* a stereotype but continually *reinvents* the category of cats. This conception of memory seems to me one of the most powerful features of the book because it provides an alternative to the traditional idea of memory as a storehouse of knowledge and experience, and of remembering as a process of retrieval from the storehouse.

2. The brain must have a system for learning. Learning for Edelman involves not only memory but also value, a way of valuing some stimuli over others. A system has to prefer some things to others in order to learn. Learning is a matter of changes in behavior that are based on categorizations governed by positive and negative values. For example, an animal might value what is light over what is dark, or what is warm over what is cold, and learning for the animal involves relating perceptual categorization and memory to such a set of values.

3. The brain also needs the ability to discriminate the self from the nonself. This is not yet self-consciousness,

because it can be done without a discrete concept of the self, but the nervous system must be able to discriminate the organism of which it is a part from the rest of the world. The apparatus for this distinction is already given to us by our brain anatomy because we have different areas of the brain for registering our internal states, such as feeling hunger, from those that take in signals from the external world, such as the visual system that enables us to see objects around us. Feeling hunger is part of the "self"; objects seen in the world around us are part of the "nonself."

These three features are necessary but not yet sufficient conditions for primary consciousness. To get the full account of primary consciousness we have to add three more elements:

4. The organism needs a system for categorizing successive events in time and for forming concepts. For example, an animal can perceive a particular event, say a cat walking across its visual field. It can then perceive another event, a dog walking across its visual field. The animal must not only be able to categorize cat and dog, but be able to categorize the sequence of events as a sequence of a cat followed by a dog. And it must be able to form prelinguistic concepts corresponding to these categories. I believe Edelman lumps these two categories together—the categorization of successive events and the formation of concepts—because he thinks they have a common neurobiological substrate in the brain.

5. A special kind of memory is needed. There must be ongoing interactions between system 4 and the systems described in 1, 2, and 3 in such a way as to give us a special memory system for values matched to past categories. Edelman gives no concrete examples, so I will try to invent one for him: suppose

an animal values warmth over cold. It relates this value to the categories of objects that have from outside the self caused the inside experiences of warmth and cold, such as, for example, the experience of sunshine for warmth and the experience of snow for cold. The animal has categories corresponding to the sequences of events that cause warmth and that cause cold. And its memories are related to ongoing perceptual categorizations in real time.

6. Finally, and most importantly, we need a set of reentrant connections between the special memory system and the anatomical systems that are dedicated to perceptual categorizations. It is the functioning of these reentrant connections that give us the sufficient conditions for the appearance of primary consciousness.

So, to summarize, on Edelman's view, in order to have consciousness the following conditions are both necessary and sufficient: the brain must have systems for categorization, and it must also have the kinds of memory Edelman describes, as well as a system for learning, where learning necessarily involves values. The brain must be able to make the distinction between the self and the rest of the world, and there must be brain structures that can order events in time. And most important of all, the brain needs global reentry pathways connecting these anatomical structures.

I do not find Edelman's prose very clear and it suffers from a lack of examples. This is the best reconstruction I can make. In his own words, he summarizes his theory as follows:

> In effect, primary consciousness results from the inter-action in real time between memories of past value

category correlations and present world input as it is categorized by global mappings (but before the components of these mappings are altered by internal states). [p. 155]

And he continues,

> Put otherwise, consciousness is an outcome of a recursively comparative memory in which previous self–nonself categorizations are *continually* related to ongoing present perceptual categorizations and their short-term succession, before such categorizations have become part of that memory. [p. 155]

Higher-order consciousness can only be developed on the basis of primary consciousness. That is, in order to develop such higher-order capacities as language and symbolism, an animal has to be conscious in the first place. Higher-order consciousness evolves when animals such as ourselves are able not only to feel and perceive but also to symbolize the self–nonself distinction—that is, to have a concept of the self—and this concept can only come through social interaction. And this development, Edelman thinks, eventually leads to the further development of syntax and semantics. These involve the ability to symbolize the relations of past, present, and future in a way that enables the animal to make plans free of its immediate present experiences.

In this summary I have left out the details of how all of this might be implemented in the actual anatomy of the brain, but Edelman is quite explicit about which brain structures he takes to be performing which functions.

So much for Edelman's apparatus for consciousness. It is a powerful one, and Edelman spends most of the book developing its implications in detail. There are chapters on memory as recategorization, space and time, concept formation, value as essential to learning, the development of language and higher-order consciousness, and mental illness, among other subjects. One of the most fascinating of his speculations is how certain mental illnesses such as schizophrenia might result from breakdowns in reentry mechanisms.

What are we to think of this as an account of consciousness? As I said, it is the most thorough and profound attempt that I have seen in the neurobiological literature to deal with the problem of consciousness. Like Crick, Edelman regards much of his theory as speculative, but so much the better. Without theses to test there is no advance in our knowledge. The main difficulty is, however, obvious: so far Edelman has given no reason why a brain that has all these features would thereby have sentience or awareness. Remember, all the features of primary consciousness that I mentioned— perceptual categorization, value, memory, etc.—are supposed to be understood only through specifying their structure and the functions they perform. We are not to think of them as already conscious. The idea is that the whole set of interlocking systems produces consciousness by way of the reentrant mappings. But as so far described, it is possible that a brain could have all these functional, behavioral features, including reentrant mapping, without thereby being conscious.

The problem is the same one we encountered before: How do you get from all these structures and their functions to the qualitative states of sentience or awareness that all of us have—what some philosophers call "qualia"? Our states of awareness when we see the color red or feel warm are qualitatively different from our states of awareness when we see the color black or feel cold. Edelman is well aware of the problem of qualia. His answer to this problem in *The Remembered Present* seems to me somewhat different from the one in *Bright Air, Brilliant Fire*, but neither seems to me to be adequate. In *The Remembered Present* he says that science cannot tell us why warm feels warm and we should not ask it to. But it seems to me that that is exactly what a neuroscience of consciousness should tell us: what anatomical and physiological features of the brain cause us to have consciousness at all, and which features cause which specific forms of conscious states. The perception of the redness of red and the warmth of warm are—among many other things—precisely the conscious states that need explaining.

In *Bright Air, Brilliant Fire*, Edelman says we cannot solve the problem of qualia because no two people will have the same qualia and there is no way that science, with its generality, can account for these peculiar and specific differences. But this does not seem to me the real difficulty. Everyone also has a different set of fingerprints from everyone else, but this does not prevent us from getting a scientific account of skin. No doubt my pains are a little bit different from yours, and perhaps we will never have a complete causal account of how and why they differ. All the same, we still need a scientific account of how exactly pains are caused by brain processes, and such an account need not worry about minute differences between one person's pain and another's. So the peculiarity of individual experience does not place the subject of individual experience outside the realm of scientific inquiry.

Any explanation of consciousness must account for subjective states of awareness, i.e., conscious states. Edelman's account is confronted with the following difficulty: either the brain's physiological features are supposed to be constitutive of consciousness—i.e., they somehow make up the state of consciousness—or they are supposed to cause consciousness. But clearly they are not constitutive of consciousness because a brain might have all these features and still be totally unconscious. So the relationship must be causal, and that interpretation is supported by Edelman's talk of necessary and sufficient conditions. But if the brain has physical structures which are supposed to cause consciousness, then we need to be told how they might do so.

How is it supposed to work? Assuming that we understand how the reentrant mechanisms cause the brain to develop unconscious categories corresponding to its stimulus inputs, how exactly do the reentrant mechanisms also cause states of awareness? One might argue that any brain sufficiently rich to have all this apparatus in operation would necessarily have to be conscious. But for such a causal hypothesis the same question remains—how does it cause consciousness? And is it really the case that brains that have these mechanisms are conscious and those that do not are not? So the mystery remains. The problem of what accounts for the inner qualitative states of awareness or sentience called "qualia" is not an aspect of the problem of consciousness that we can set on one side; it *is* the problem of consciousness, because every conscious state is a qualitative state, and "qualia" is just a misleading name for the consciousness of all conscious states.

Edelman has written two brilliant books, both of them rich in ideas. He discusses with remarkable erudition topics ranging from quantum mechanics to computer science to schizophrenia, and often his insights are dazzling. One impressive feature of his theory is its detailed attempt to specify which neuronal structures in the brain are responsible for which functions. Though Edelman differs from Crick on many issues, they share the one basic conviction that drives their research. To understand the mind and consciousness we are going to have to understand in detail how the brain works.

Chapter Four

Roger Penrose, Kurt Gödel, and the Cytoskeletons

1.

All of the works I am considering deal in one way or another with the relations between consciousness and the brain. Crick, Edelman, and Israel Rosenfield think, as I do, that brain processes —probably at the levels of neurons, synapses, and neuronal groups—cause consciousness. Dennett and Chalmers think that brains are just one type of computational or information-processing device that can sustain consciousness.[1] Roger Penrose's book *Shadows of the Mind*[2] is also about brains and consciousness, but it is written at a much more abstract level than any of the others. It is not until after three hundred and fifty pages that there is any serious discussion of brain anatomy and there is very little discussion of the special features of consciousness anywhere in the book.

---

1. Strictly speaking, Dennett ends up by denying the real existence of consciousness, as we will see in chapter 5.
2. *Shadows of the Mind: A Search for the Missing Science of Consciousness* (Oxford University Press, 1994).

Why is Penrose's approach so different? He believes he has good reasons for the larger angle of vision with which he surveys the field. The standard discussions, he believes, neglect the special bearing of two of the most important intellectual achievements of the twentieth century: quantum mechanics and Gödel's theorem, which shows that there are statements in mathematical systems which are true but which cannot be proven within those systems. The usual discussions, my own included, assume that the computer can be used at least to simulate or model mental processes and they assume that the sorts of neurobiological processes that I described in the previous chapter are the right phenomena to explain consciousness. Penrose thinks that if we understood the implications of Gödel's theorem and the importance of quantum mechanics for the study of the mind, we would reject both of these assumptions.

Other authors try to describe consciousness and to describe how the brain works to cause consciousness. Penrose emphatically does not plunge into any discussion of either brain or consciousness. He concentrates first on Gödel's theorem and then on quantum mechanics, because he thinks we cannot intelligently discuss consciousness or its relations to either brains or computers without first understanding these deeper issues. If Penrose is right, most of the contemporary discussions of the relation between consciousness and the brain are hopelessly misconceived. Penrose's aim is to establish this, and we have to keep this aim in mind when we examine his complex and convoluted arguments.

Shadows of the Mind is a sequel to his earlier *The Emperor's New Mind*[3] and many of the same points are made,

---

3. *The Emperor's New Mind: Concerning Computers, Minds, and the Laws of Physics* (Oxford University Press, 1989).

with further developments and answers to objections to his earlier book. *Shadows of the Mind* divides into two equal parts. In the first he uses a variation of Gödel's famous proof of the incompleteness of mathematical systems to try to prove that we are not computers and cannot even be simulated on computers. Not only is Strong AI false, Weak AI is too. In the second half he provides a lengthy explanation of quantum mechanics with some speculations on how a quantum mechanical theory of the brain might explain consciousness in a way that he thinks classical physics cannot possibly explain it. This, by the way, is the only book I know where you can find lengthy and clear explanations of both of these two great discoveries, Gödel's incompleteness theorem and quantum mechanics.

Before getting into the details of his argument, I would like to situate it in relation to the current discussions of computational attempts at simulation of human cognition. There has never been a time when more nonsense was talked about computers than the present era. Here is an example. Recently a chess-playing program, Deep Blue, was able to beat the very best of the world's grandmasters at chess. What psychological significance should we attach to such a program? There was in the press a great deal of discussion about how this might be a threat to human dignity or some such, but if you know what a computer is, and you know what these programs do, you will not be tempted to any such spectacular conclusion. A computer is a device that manipulates symbols. We have invented forms of electronics that enable the device to manipulate the symbols very rapidly, millions of manipulations per second. In the case of the chess-playing computers, we can encode our representations of chess moves into the meaningless symbols in the computer. We can program the computer so that it processes these symbols very rapidly, and then we can get it to print out instructions which we decode as being about chess. But the computer knows nothing of chess, moves, pieces, or anything else. It just manipulates meaningless formal symbols according to the instructions we give it.

When asked by the news media if I thought human dignity was threatened by Deep Blue, I pointed out that it was no more threatened by it than by the fact that pocket calculators can outperform any mathematician, or that mechanical ditch diggers can outperform any person with a shovel. Some computational programs try to mimic the formal features of human cognition. But the recent chess-playing programs do not even do that. These programs succeed by what is known as "brute force." In response to the moves of their opponents they are able to calculate millions of possible moves, 200 million moves per second, in a way that is totally unlike the thought processes of any actual chess player. So, there are two reasons why Deep Blue, though no doubt a wonderful programming achievement, is not a piece of human or superhuman psychology. First, like any other digital computer it works by manipulating meaningless symbols. The only meaning the symbols have is what we as outside interpreters attach to them. Second, the chess-playing programs don't even try to simulate human psychology. They just use the brute computational power of modern electronics to defeat the opponent.[4]

More recently *The New York Times* reported that new

4. For details see Monty Newborn, *Kasparov versus Deep Blue: Computer Chess Comes of Age* (Springer, 1997).

mathematical theorem–proving programs can now do something very much like genuine reasoning. But once again, this "genuine reasoning" is, from the computer's point of view, simply a matter of manipulating meaningless symbols. We have found ways to program computers so that they can prove theorems and sometimes produce results that even the programmer would not have predicted. This is a remarkable achievement on the part of the programmers and the engineers, but it is a matter of simulating certain human cognitive capacities; and as we saw in our discussion of the Chinese Room Argument, simulation should not be confused with duplication. Anybody who knows the definition of the computer, the definition that Alan Turing gave half a century ago, knows that the modern digital computer is a device for manipulating formal symbols, normally thought of as zeroes and ones. These symbols are meaningless until some outside human programmer or user attaches an interpretation to them.

"But," so a common objection goes, "should we not think of the brain as also manipulating zeroes and ones, because neurons are in a sense binary? They either fire or don't. And if the brain operates in a binary code, then surely the brain must be a digital computer too." Several things are wrong with this analogy, but the most important is this: the crucial difference between the neurons and the symbols in the computer is that the neurons act *causally* to cause consciousness and other mental phenomena by specific biological mechanisms. But the zeroes and ones are purely abstract. Their only causal power is the power of the implementing medium, the hardware, to produce the next stage of the program when the machine is running. Neurons can indeed be *simulated* by a computer program, but the simulation of neuron firings no more guarantees the power of neurons to cause consciousness than the computer simulation of a rainstorm or five-alarm fires guarantees the causal powers of rain or fire. The brain simulator program by itself no more causes consciousness than the fire simulator program burns the house down or the rain simulator program leaves us all drenched.

Now, all of these points are familiar to Penrose. I believe he would not disagree with anything I have just said. But he wants to go further to show that there are things that conscious human beings can do that computers cannot even simulate. Granted the distinction between a mere computational simulation of consciousness and actually duplicating the power of the brain to cause consciousness, Penrose thinks there are some features of consciousness that cannot even be simulated. He grants that computers can play chess and prove mathematical theorems but he thinks there are some things conscious agents can do that computers cannot do.

Penrose begins his book by distinguishing four possible positions about the relation of computation to consciousness:

A. Strong AI. Consciousness and other mental phenomena consist entirely in computational processes.
B. Weak AI. Brain processes cause consciousness, and these processes can be simulated on a computer. But the computational simulation by itself does not guarantee consciousness.
C. Brain processes cause consciousness but these processes "cannot even be properly simulated computationally" (p. 12).

D. Consciousness cannot be explained scientifically by any means, computational or otherwise.

He rejects A, Strong AI, just as I do; but unlike me he rejects B also. He wants to argue for the much stronger position, C. On his view, even Weak AI is false. D is an antiscientific position, which he wants to reject and to distinguish from C. Why does he think it is important to argue for C, if A is acknowledged to be false, and computation by itself is not enough for consciousness? Because, he says, science adopts an "operational viewpoint," and if you could program a computer to behave exactly like a human it would be scientifically tempting to think that it had mental states just as a human does. Penrose wants to show that you cannot have such a program. The external manifestations of consciousness in the form of human behavior cannot be simulated computationally, and indeed since the brain is causally responsible for that behavior, the brain cannot be simulated either. Because brain and body are physical it follows that not all physical processes can be simulated computationally; particularly those involving consciousness cannot be simulated. Throughout this book, Penrose has surprisingly little to say about consciousness. He is concerned rather with its "external manifestations" in physical behavior, particularly its manifestations in the activities of mathematical reasoning, as we will see.

The book is long and difficult, but the overall structure of the argument is as follows (this is my summary, not his):

1. Gödel's theorem proves that there are true statements in mathematical systems which are not provable as theorems of the system.

2. A specific version of Gödel's theorem, the unsolvability of the halting problem, can be used to prove that our conscious behavior cannot even be simulated on a computer. The halting problem, as we will see, is a purely abstract mathematical problem concerning the possibility of getting a set of mathematical procedures that will determine whether a computation will stop (or halt). (For example, if we program our computer to start with the sequence 1, 2, 3, . . . and find a number larger than 8, it will stop on 9; but if we ask it to find an odd number that is the sum of two even numbers it will never stop, because there is no such number. The proof demonstrates that there are some nonstopping computational procedures that cannot be shown to be nonstopping by computational methods but we can nonetheless see that they are nonstopping. For details see the appendix to this chapter.)

3. Neurons are computable, i.e., their various features can be computationally simulated. Therefore, they cannot explain consciousness, because consciousness has features that are not computable, and neurons are computable.

4. To explain consciousness we require something "genuinely noncomputable." This will have to be at the subneuronal level, probably the level of the microtubules in the neurons. To understand this will require a revolution in physics.

In what follows I will explain Penrose's arguments for 2, 3, and 4 and try to show that none of them is established by his arguments.

It is perhaps important to emphasize that Penrose is not saying that no mathematical processes done by conscious humans can be simulated on a computer. Of course they can. Many of the things that mathematicians do, and indeed just about all the mathematical operations that ordinary people do, can be simulated on computers. Penrose is only eager to insist that there are some areas of conscious human thinking, as particularly exemplified by Gödel's theorem, that cannot be simulated on a computer. To repeat, he is not saying that none of our mathematical abilities are simulatable, but rather that not all of them are. The argument is entirely about certain arcane areas of mathematics. He says (in conversation) that he emphasizes mathematics because that is what he knows most about. But he thinks perhaps similar arguments could be brought forward about music, art, or other conscious human activities. It is just that as a mathematician he wants to show that not *all* of his mathematical abilities can be simulated on a computer. And the fact that 99.9 percent of his abilities can be simulated is irrelevant. For Penrose, if you can get just one counterexample to Weak AI, this constitutes a total refutation.

2.

The first version of the Gödel argument against computationalism goes back to an article by John R. Lucas, an Oxford philosopher, published in the early Sixties.[5] Lucas argued that Gödel had shown that there are statements in mathematical

---

5. "Minds, Machines and Gödel," in *Philosophy*, Vol. 36 (1961), pp. 112–127. Reprinted in A. R. Anderson, *Minds and Machines* (Prentice Hall, 1964).

systems that cannot be proven as theorems within those systems, but which we can see to be true. A theorem of a system is any statement that follows logically from the axioms of the system. Lucas gives the following sort of example. Suppose we had a list of statements in some formal system numbered 1, 2, 3, etc. And suppose statement number 17 is about itself. Suppose it says,

17. Statement number 17 is not provable in this system.

We can see that 17 is true, because to assume it is false is to assume a self-contradiction. To assume that it is provable that it is not provable is to assume that it both is and is not provable. We can therefore see that 17 is true, and because true, not provable.

Common sense would tell us that there is something fishy here because there seems to be no substance to statement 17. What is the substance supposed to be that is provable or not provable? However, that is not how most mathematicians or logicians think. They think that as far as substance is concerned, statement 17 is just fine. As a piece of standard mathematical-logical English, there is nothing wrong with statement 17. It just says of itself that it is not provable. That is its only substance. Gödel's examples are much more complex than this, as we will see, but they rely on the same principle of providing cases which we can see to be true but which are not provable.

It follows from such examples, according to Lucas, that our understanding exceeds that of any computer. A computer uses only algorithms—sets of precise rules that specify a sequence of actions to be taken in order to solve a problem or prove a proposition. Hence when a computer proves a theorem it must use a theorem-proving algorithm. But there are some statements that we can see to be true that are not provable in the system. Such statements are therefore not theorems of the system and are therefore not provable by a theorem-proving algorithm. It follows, according to Lucas, that our knowledge of those truths cannot be algorithmic. But since computers use only algorithms (a program is an algorithm), it follows that we are not computers.

There were many objections to Lucas's argument, but an obvious one is this: from the fact that our knowledge of these truths does not come by way of a theorem-proving algorithm it does not follow that we use no algorithms at all in arriving at these conclusions. Not all algorithms are theorem-proving algorithms. For example, in cognitive science, a program that simulates vision will typically have an algorithm for constructing a three-dimensional description of the visual field from the description of the two-dimensional array of stimuli on the retina.[6] That algorithm will specify, for example, how the stimulus on the retina produces a visual image of an object. But the algorithm that proceeds from the retinal stimulus to the three-dimensional description does not prove any theorems. Similarly, in the sort of case discussed by Lucas, we might have an algorithm that enables us to see that a statement that says of itself that it is not provable as a theorem in some system can't be provable as a theorem in that system, and hence is true, even though its truth cannot be established by a theorem-proving algorithm in that system. It is possible, in short, that we are using some computational procedure that is

---

6. See David Marr, *Vision* (W. H. Freeman and Co., 1982).

not a theorem-proving procedure.

This is, I believe, a fairly standard style of objection to the Lucas argument. Penrose revives the argument with a beautiful version of Gödel's proof, one that was first made by Alan Turing, and is usually called "the proof of the unsolvability of the halting problem." The halting problem, as I said earlier, is a purely abstract mathematical problem of finding a set of mathematical procedures which would determine for any computation whether or not it will stop (or halt). Since even I, a nonmathematician, think I can understand this argument, and since we are not going to be able to assess its philosophical significance if we don't try to understand it, I summarize it in the appendix to this chapter for those willing to try to follow it.

How exactly does Penrose use the unsolvability of the halting problem to prove we are not computers? That is not as easy a question to answer as it ought to be. In the actual text of his book (p. 75ff.) he says that as long as we *know* of a set of computational procedures A that it is sound then we know that there are some computations, $C_k(k)$, that do not stop. (A computation $C_k(k)$ would be the kth computation performed on the number k. So, if k equals 8, then $C_k(k)$ would be the eighth computation on the number 8.) But the proof of the unsolvability of the halting problem demonstrates that the set of computational algorithms A is insufficient to ascertain that the computation $C_k(k)$ does not stop. So A cannot encapsulate our understanding. Since A can be any set of computational algorithms, it follows that we are not computers carrying out an algorithm. He summarizes this conclusion as follows:

We deduce that no knowably sound set of computational rules (such as A) can ever suffice for ascertaining that computations do not stop, since there are some non-stopping computations (such as $C_k(k)$) that must elude these rules. Moreover, since from the knowledge of A and of its soundness, we can actually construct a computation $C_k(k)$ that we can *see* does not ever stop, we deduce that A *cannot* be a formalization of the procedures available to mathematicians for ascertaining that computations do not stop, no matter what A is. [pp. 75–76]

Therefore

Human mathematicians are not using a knowably sound algorithm in order to ascertain mathematical truth. [p. 76]

(It is perhaps worth repeating that he is not claiming that mathematicians never use algorithms. Of course, most of the time they do. His point is that some of the time they do something more.)

In a subsequent debate over the book in the internet journal *Psyche*[7] he gives a slightly different version. In this version, he does not explicitly require that the algorithm be "knowably sound." He simply hypothesizes that our human mathematical abilities are encapsulated in some algorithm or

---

7. "Beyond the Doubting of a Shadow: A Reply to Commentaries on Shadows of the Mind," in *Psyche: An Interdisciplinary Journal of Research on Consciousness* 2(23), January 1996, http://psyche.cs.monash.edu.au.

other and then he derives a contradiction from that hypothesis. In short, he presents a *reductio ad absurdum* argument: assume I am a computer carrying out a computer algorithm and you will be able to derive a contradiction from that assumption. I think the *Psyche* version is the most succinct statement of his argument, and I will now summarize it.

Assume that the totality of methods of humanly accessible, unassailable mathematical reasoning is encapsulated in some formal system F. F will include but need not be confined to a set of true axioms and a set of inference rules, which give valid inferences. In addition to such "top-down" methods it can also include any "bottom-up" computational methods you care to put in. Top-down methods would include such higher-level phenomena as principles of logical reasoning and mathematical axioms. Bottom-up methods would include algorithms that simulate lower-level brain processes that underlie our mathematical reasoning. An idealized mathematician confronted with F might wonder, Penrose writes, "Am I F?" where that just means, "Does F encapsulate all the humanly accessible methods of mathematical proof?" Now such a mathematician confronted with F could reason as follows: I don't necessarily know that I am F but if I am then it is both the case that F is sound and that the conjunction of F and the claim that I am F is also sound. Call that conjunction F'. From the assumption that I am F it follows that the Gödel statement to the effect that the computation does not stop—a statement we can call $G(F')$—is true. I can just see that it is true. But it is not a consequence of F': that is, I can see that if I happen to be F then the Gödel statement $G(F')$ is true; as soon as I understand it I can see that it is true. But perceptions of this sort are precisely what F' was supposed to be able to achieve, and F' cannot achieve such perceptions. It cannot do so because the truth in question is not a consequence of F'. Therefore I cannot be F after all.

In short the supposition that I am F, where F is any "Gödelizable" set of computational procedures, leads to a contradiction. I can perceive the truth of statements which go beyond the powers of F and that contradicts the claim that F encapsulates all my powers. This argument works for any candidate for F.

What are we to make of Penrose's arguments? A number of logicians, philosophers, and computer scientists have objected on more or less technical grounds. A common objection made to the original argument was this: from the fact that no "knowably sound" algorithm can account for our mathematical abilities it does not follow that there could not be an algorithm which we did not and perhaps even could not know to be correct which accounted for those abilities. Suppose that we are following a program unconsciously and that it is so long and complicated that we could never grasp the whole thing at once. We can understand each step, but there are so many thousands of steps we could never grasp the whole program at once. That is, Penrose's argument rests on what we can know and understand, but it is not a requirement of computational cognitive science that people be able to understand the programs they are supposed to be using to solve cognitive problems.

This objection was made, for example, by Hilary Putnam in his review of Penrose in *The New York Times Book Review*. Penrose's argument, said Putnam, "is a straightforward case of a mathematical fallacy." Penrose responded with two indignant letters.[8] Penrose has long been aware of this objection and discussed it at some length in his book. In fact, he considers and answers in detail some twenty different objections to his argument (pp. 77–116). His aim is to show that any unknowable, unconscious algorithm can be reduced to a consciously knowable one. He argues, for example, that as long as the algorithm is finite, then each step is knowable and understandable, but if each step is knowable and understandable then eventually all the steps can come to be known and understood (p. 133 ff.).

Penrose's point can best be illustrated with the example of robots. If the AI project of building a robot able to do human-level mathematics succeeded, then—according to Penrose—human-level mathematics would necessarily be reducible to a theorem-proving procedure, because a robot could use only theorem-proving procedures. But the assumption that human-level mathematics is reducible to a theorem-proving procedure is precisely what leads to the contradiction he describes. The robot, using only theorem-proving procedures, could not grasp the truth of the Gödel sentence, but I am able to grasp its truth. Therefore my abilities cannot be encapsulated in the robot's theorem-proving procedures.

Therefore he concludes that at least some of the external manifestations of consciousness are different from the external manifestations of computation.

---

8. *The New York Times Book Review*, November 20, 1994, p. 7; December 18, 1994, p. 39; and January 15, 1995, p. 31.

3.

So far it seems to me that Penrose is winning the argument. I realize that many mathematical logicians and philosophers remain unconvinced, but I do not believe his argument stands or falls on the possibility that we are using unknown algorithms we cannot understand. In any case, in his *Psyche* article he tries to sidestep the issue. In my discussion I am going to assume that Penrose is right that this style of objection is not damaging to his case. What has he proven? Has he proven that Weak AI is impossible?

No, he has not. I believe that the fallacy in Penrose's argument can be stated quite simply: from the fact that a certain type of computational simulation cannot be given of a process under one description it does not follow that another type of computational simulation cannot be given of the very same process under another description. I will present some examples of how this might work. Remember the latest version of his argument. Take the totality of "*methods of mathematical reasoning.*" Call them *F*. Now I wonder if I am *F*. From the supposition that I am *F* and that *F* is sound (call the conjunction of these suppositions *F'*) I can see that the Gödel sentence *G(F')* is true, but the truth of the Gödel sentence does not follow from *F'*. So the assumption that I am *F* generates a contradiction. So I cannot be *F*.

So far so good. But what the argument shows is that I cannot be simulated at the level of mathematical reasoning by a program that uses only sound methods of mathematical proof. But the conclusion Penrose draws is that I cannot be simulated *under any description whatever* of the processes by which I see the truth of the Gödel sentences. That conclusion does not follow. Penrose's conclusion only follows as long as we confine our simulations to "methods of mathematical reasoning." And the argument if valid shows only that I cannot be F, where F is designed to capture every method of mathematical reasoning, whether top-down or bottom-up. Penrose's argument shows that I cannot be simulated by a program that simulates F, but not all computer simulations have to take the form of F.

An intelligent version of Weak AI should attempt to simulate actual cognitive processes. Now, one way to simulate cognitive processes is to simulate brain processes. These brain simulations have no normative character at all. They include, for example, simulations of the processes that produce perceptual illusions. The questions of soundness, validity, etc., do not even arise for these simulations any more than they arise for simulations of the weather or digestive processes. The simulations just simulate a bunch of brute, blind, neurological processes, those that underlie our mathematical and other sorts of reasoning. But to repeat this essential point, there is no question of soundness or unsoundness. The neurological processes are not even possible candidates for being judged as sound or unsound.

Consider a trivial program first. Using the standard binary symbols 0 and 1, let 0 stand for "Penrose (or an idealized mathematician) is thinking about the truth of the Gödel sentences," and let 1 stand for "Penrose sees its truth." Then Program One says, go from state 0 to state 1. This is a perfect simulation of Penrose's mathematical reasoning. He would agree but is not troubled by the example. It is, he says (in a letter he sent me) "hardly a 'simulation of his cognitive processes,'" because it is too trivial and does not explain anything. I agree that it is trivial, but it ought already to be worrying because all that any digital computer program has is a finite sequence of just such trivialities. Any computer program for anything consists in precisely a series of such discrete states expressed in a binary notation. One of the aims of AI is to reduce complex mental processes to just such trivial steps as this. So let's go a bit deeper. If we make the reasonable assumption, which I take it Penrose would accept, that there is a strict correlation between brain processes and thought processes, there will be two brain processes, one corresponding to Penrose thinking about the Gödel sentence and wondering whether it is true and the other to Penrose seeing it is true. Call those brain processes X and Y. A parallel program to Program One is Program Two: go from state X to state Y. "X" and "Y" here refer to states of the brain described entirely in terms of neuron firings, transmitters, etc. They say nothing about thinking, but someone who knew independently that there was a strict correlation and who knew how Penrose's brain worked could read off the thought processes from the descriptions of X and Y. To put this point differently, the same sequence of events in the brain can be described with or without mentioning its mental content.

Okay, Program Two is just as dumb and trivial as Program One. So let's go to Program Three. There is a whole conglomeration of thought processes by which Penrose comes to see the truth of the Gödel sentences. Suppose he does it in one hundred steps (or a thousand or a million, it doesn't matter). Corresponding to those steps will be an exactly parallel set of brain processes, B_1, B_2, B_3, B_4. . . . And suppose further that we have a program that says: go from B_1 to B_2 to B_3 until you get to B_{100} and then go to Y. Now notice that the steps in this program and the corresponding steps in the brain say nothing whatever about "methods of mathematical reasoning," "truth judgments," "soundness," or any of the rest of the mathematical apparatus. It is just one bunch of neuron firings followed by another bunch. It is just brute, blind, neurobiological processes all the way down and from beginning to end. Absolutely nothing is said about methods of mathematical reasoning, though anyone who knew *independently* of the correlations could read off the thought processes from the brain processes.

Penrose's argument shows that there cannot be a computational simulation at the level of *mathematical reasoning*. Fine, but it does not follow that there cannot be computational simulation of the very same sequence of events at the level of brain processes, and we know that there must be such a level of brain processes because we know that any mathematical reasoning must be realized in the brain. Not only all neurobiologists but Penrose himself would agree that any change in mental states must be perfectly matched by a change in brain states. Notice that we do not need to suppose that the type of brain state is always the same for any two mathematicians having the same mathematical thought. Perhaps the specific instances of the brain realization in different brains are different even for the same type of thought. That does not matter for this argument, which only requires that for any actual event of mathematical reasoning going on in the mind of a mathematician, there must be some brain realization of that event. So Penrose does not show that there is no nontrivial simulation of his brain processes when he sees the truth of the Gödel sentences.

Penrose thinks he blocks this sort of argument when he includes bottom-up as well as top-down methods of mathematical reasoning in F. Bottom-up methods of reasoning would be at the microlevel in the brain, but Penrose thinks that he can get some methods of mathematical reasoning that guarantee truth at this level. However, in what I have called Program Three there are no methods of mathematical reasoning at all, neither top-down nor bottom-up. The elements referred to by Program Three will be such things as "The neurotransmitter serotonin is secreted into the synaptic clefts of 87 neurons in prefrontal cortical cell assembly number 391X." So there can be no question of "soundness" or any other evaluation. The basic difference between F and Program Three is that F is normative. It sets normative standards of mathematical reasoning that are supposed to guarantee mathematical truth. But there is nothing normative about brute, blind brain processes and correspondingly there is nothing normative in the programs that simulate those processes.

Now it might be objected, and I think Penrose would object, that such a simulation as I have proposed does not guarantee truth judgments. It does not guarantee mathematical truth. Such a claim would be correct but it is not an objection. Actual brain processes do not *guarantee* truth either. Real live brains are empirical, material objects and their behavior can be simulated as can the behavior of any other material phenomena, whether they be rainstorms, earthquakes, or mathematical understanders. Or, at any rate, if their behavior cannot be simulated, Penrose has not so far demonstrated this fact.

But what about his argument concerning robots? Penrose agrees, of course, that a computer and, a fortiori, a robot, could do some mathematical reasoning. But he thinks he has shown that you could not program a robot to do all the mathematical reasoning that human beings are capable of. But once again that claim has to be qualified. He has, if he is right, shown that you could not program a robot to do human-level mathematical reasoning if you programmed it solely with algorithmic mathematical reasoning programs. But suppose you programmed it with totally nonnormative brain simulator programs. There is no question of "truth judgments" or "soundness" in the programs. Nothing in his argument shows that "human-level mathematical reasoning" could not emerge as a product of the robot's brain simulator program, just as it emerges as a product of actual human brains. I think the idea is a science fiction fantasy, but the point I am making now is that he has not shown that it is in principle impossible.

Penrose's key claim is that any robot that could simulate human-level mathematics would have to have a program reducible to a theorem-producing procedure; but that claim is only correct for programs that simulate mathematical reasoning. The programs I have described, Programs One, Two, and Three, simulate no mathematical reasoning at all, neither top-down nor bottom-up. They simulate nonnormative brain correlates of mathematical reasoning. *Just as the human brain uses mathematical algorithms but does not consist in those algorithms, so the simulation of the human brain uses mathematical algorithms but does not consist in those algorithms.*

I want to hammer this point home, because it is the simplest way to state my objection to Penrose. In his book he has a fantasy dialogue with a theorem-proving robot (pp. 179–190). The robot has been programmed with theorem-proving algorithms and it boasts about its mathematical ability ("We don't make the kind of stupid mistakes that humans occasionally make in their firm mathematical assertions," [p. 181]), but Penrose is able to demonstrate that humans can do something that the robot cannot do. Human beings can see the truth of the Gödel sentences, but the robot cannot see that. I think the fact that Penrose imagines a robot that exceeds human abilities shows he has not understood Weak AI as an attempt to *simulate actual human cognition.* I now want to imagine a different kind of robot from the one Penrose imagines, one that is a simulation of real human beings. My robot says, "I am liable to make exactly the same sorts of mistakes that humans make, because my brain has been programmed to simulate their brains. I have been programmed with no theorem-proving algorithms at all, but I can still do mathematics the same as humans, because my mathematical abilities result from my brain simulator algorithms, just as human mathematical abilities result from the physical properties of their actual brains."

Let us try to state seriously the principles underlying the construction of such a robot. If we want to build a robot to do what humans do, we first need to state what humans are and how they do what they do. For mathematical purposes humans are *identical with* their brains, and their brains *use*, but are not identical with, mathematical algorithms. So in our robot we will have programs that exactly simulate brain processes and these programs will use mathematical algorithms. For mathematical purposes the robot will be *identical with* its brain simulator programs and these programs will *use*, but not be identical with, mathematical algorithms.

Such a robot, if it were accurately programmed, would be able in practice to do what mathematicians do. It would make the sort of mistakes that mathematicians make, and it would get the sort of correct results that mathematicians get. Indeed after a while the robot will be able to offer a Penrose-style proof that it is not identical with the mathematical algorithms it uses. The proof goes:

> Take any set of mathematical algorithms A, together with my knowledge of A and that it is sound. From this I can construct computations that I can see do not stop. But A by itself is insufficient to demonstrate that these computations do not stop. It follows that A is not a formalization of my procedures for figuring out that computations do not stop. Etc. . . .

Notice that the robot does not need to be conscious to do any of this. The proof might just appear as a computer printout, resulting from the nonconscious operations of the robot's computer brain, in the same way that the computer on which I am writing this produces complex printouts that do not require consciousness in the computer. Indeed, it is hard to see any essential connection between Penrose's argument about Gödel and the problem of consciousness. Nowhere does he explain why an unconscious being could not produce all of his arguments.

But what about the possibility of errors? Of my robot, one can say, as one can say about any human mathematician, perhaps it will make errors, perhaps not. Whether or not it *in fact* makes errors is beside the point. The point is that the computational rules that constitute its program are not such as to give a mathematical *guarantee* of mathematical truth. That is to say, they are not, in Penrose's sense, sound. In that sense, the issue of errors is quite beside the point. If there were in fact a mathematician who never made errors, that mathematician would still have a brain, and its processes would consist of brute, blind, neurophysiological processes for which the question of soundness doesn't arise. A computational simulation of that mathematician would simulate those processes. The processes might in practice never make a mistake, but the brain simulator programs that enable it to get the right answers are not mathematical guarantees of truth. Like the brain of our imagined mathematician, they just happen to work in practice.

Gödel's theorem rests on an ingenious formal maneuver. There is nothing wrong with that. Many results in mathematics and logic rely on ingenious maneuvers. But the formal maneuver does not have the consequences for computer simulations that Penrose and Lucas think. To appreciate this consider a parallel maneuver. Suppose someone said, "Computers can never predict all of human behavior, for suppose a computer predicted Jones will produce the first occurrence of the sentence 'I just ate Mt. Everest with ketchup on it.' Then the computer itself would have just produced the first occurrence of the sentence and so the prediction would be false." This argument is fallacious because someone can produce a prediction which describes that sentence without actually producing it; that is, the prediction identifies the sentence but under another description, e.g., "The sentence which begins with the capital of the ninth letter of the alphabet...etc." In spite of all its mathematical sophistication, Penrose's argument rests on a similar fallacy. From the fact that we cannot simulate a process at the level of, and under the description, "theorem proving" or "mathematical reasoning" it does not follow that we cannot simulate the very same process, with the same predictions, at some other level and under another description.

To summarize this argument: Penrose fails to distinguish between normative algorithms that are supposed to provide "unassailable mathematical reasoning" and the sorts of algorithms that just simulate natural processes such as rainstorms or cellular mechanisms. Nothing in his argument shows that the second kind of algorithm is impossible where brain processes are concerned. The real objection to the second kind of algorithm is not one he makes. It is that such computer models don't really explain anything, because the algorithms play no *causal* role in the behavior of the brain. They simply provide simulations or models or representations of what is happening.

4.

In the second part of his book, Penrose summarizes the current state of our knowledge of quantum mechanics and tries to apply its lessons to the problem of consciousness. Much of this is difficult to read, but among the relatively nontechnical accounts of quantum mechanics that I have seen this seems to me the clearest. If you have ever wanted to know about superposition, the collapse of the wave function, the paradox of

Schrödinger's cat, and the Einstein-Podolsky-Rosen phenomena, this may be the best place to find out.

But what has all this to do with consciousness? Penrose's speculation is that the computable world of classical physics is unable to account for the noncomputational character of the mind, that is, the features of the mind which he thinks cannot even be simulated on a computer. But he thinks that a noncomputable version of quantum mechanics might be able to do the job. Thus the logical structure of his book is as follows: in the first half he argues that Gödel's theorem shows that there are mental processes that are noncomputable, and what he thinks is true of the Gödel results, he thinks is true of consciousness in general. Consciousness is noncomputable because human consciousness is capable of achieving things that computation cannot achieve; for example, with our consciousness we can see the truth of Gödel sentences and such truths are not computable.

Then in the second half of the book he argues that some new version of quantum mechanics, some noncomputable quantum mechanics, could provide the solution to the problem of consciousness. According to Penrose, though a quantum mechanical computer would have some random features because quantum mechanics has elements of indeterminacy, even such a computer with its random features would not be able to account for the essentially noncomputational aspects of human consciousness. A quantum mechanical computer, though containing random elements, in principle at least could be simulated by an ordinary computer with some randomizing feature built in. So even a quantum mechanical computer "would not be able to perform the operations required for human

conscious understanding" (p. 356), because such understanding is not computable. But Penrose hopes that when the
physics of quantum mechanics is eventually completed, when
we have a satisfactory theory of quantum gravity, it "would
lead us to something *genuinely* non-computable" (p. 356).

And how is this supposed to work in the brain? According
to Penrose, we cannot find the answer to the problem of consciousness at the level of neurons because they are too big; they
are already objects explainable by classical physics and are
thus computable. Penrose thinks that because neurons are
computable, they cannot explain consciousness, which is noncomputable. We must look to the inner structure of the neuron and there we find a structure called a "cytoskeleton,"
which is the framework that holds the cell together and is the
control system for its operation. The cytoskeleton contains
small tubelike structures called "microtubules" (figs. 4a and
4b), and these according to Penrose have a crucial role in the
functioning of synapses (pp. 364–365). Here is the hypothesis he presents:

> On the view that I am tentatively putting forward,
> consciousness would be some manifestation of this
> quantum-entangled internal cytoskeletal state and of its
> involvement in the interplay... between quantum and
> classical levels of activity. [p. 376]

In other words the cytoskeletal stuff is all mixed up with
quantum mechanical phenomena, and when this microlevel
gets involved with the macrolevel of neurons, etc., consciousness emerges. Neurons are not on the right level to explain

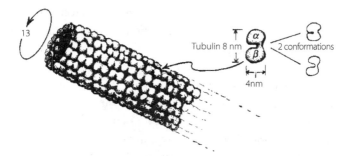

Fig. 4a. A microtubule. It is a hollow tube, normally consisting of 13 columns of tubulin dimers. Each tubulin molecule is capable of (at least) two conformations

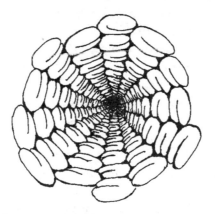

Fig. 4b. View down a microtubule! The 5 + 8 spiral arrangement of the tubulins in this microtubule can be seen

consciousness. Neurons might be just a "*magnifying device*" for the real action which is at the cytoskeletal level. The neuronal level of description might be "a mere *shadow*" of the deeper level where we have to seek the physical basis of the mind (p. 376).

What are we to make of this? I do not object to its speculative character, because at this point any account of consciousness is bound to contain speculative elements. The problem with these speculations is that they do not adequately speculate on how it is even conceivable that we might solve the problem of consciousness. They are of the form: *if* we had a better theory of quantum mechanics and *if* that theory were noncomputable then maybe we could account for consciousness in a noncomputational way. But how? It is not enough to say that the mystery of consciousness might be solved if we had a quantum mechanics even more mysterious than the present one. How could it possibly work? What are the causal mechanisms supposed to be?

There are several attempts beside Penrose's to give a quantum mechanical account of consciousness.[9] The standard complaint is that these accounts, in effect, want to substitute two mysteries for one. Penrose is unique in that he wants to add a third. To the mysteries of consciousness and quantum mechanics he wants to add a third mysterious element, a yet-to-be-discovered noncomputable quantum mechanics. Penrose answers this objection by saying that it is too much to ask him to solve all the problems. I agree that such a demand would be excessive, but the complaint is not that he does not solve all the problems, but rather that it is not at all clear how his proposal *could* solve the one that matters. How is it even conceivable that his hypothetical quantum mechanics could cause conscious processes? What might the causal mechanisms be?

9. For example, Henry P. Stapp, *Mind, Matter, and Quantum Mechanics* (Springer, 1993).

In any case the motivation for his whole line of reasoning is based on a fallacy. Let's suppose for the sake of the argument that Penrose is right that there is *no* level of description at which consciousness can be simulated. It still does not follow logically that the explanation of consciousness must for that reason be given with reference to entities that cannot be simulated. From the proposition that consciousness cannot be simulated on a computer it does not follow that the entities which cause consciousness cannot be simulated on a computer. More generally, there is no problem whatever in supposing that a set of relations that are noncomputable at some level of description can be the result of processes that are computable at some other level. Here is an example. Every registered car in California has both a vehicle identification number (VIN) and a license plate number (LPN). For registered cars there is a perfect match: for every LPN there is a VIN and vice versa, and this match continues indefinitely into the future because as new cars are manufactured each gets a VIN, and as they come into use in California each is assigned a LPN. But there is no way to compute one from the other. To put this in mathematical jargon, if we construe each series as potentially infinite, the function from VIN to LPN is a noncomputable function. But so what? Noncomputability by itself is of little significance and does not imply that the processes that produce the noncomputable relations must therefore be noncomputable. For all I know, the assignment of VINs at the car factories may be done by computer, and if it isn't, it certainly could be. The assignment of LPNs ideally is done by one of the oldest algorithms known: first come, first served.

The upshot of these considerations is to reinforce the conclusion we reached in our discussion of Penrose's Gödel argument.

The question "Is consciousness computable?" only makes sense relative to some specific feature or function of consciousness and at some specific level of description. And even if you have some specific function that is noncomputable, my seeing the truth of Gödel sentences for example, it does not follow that the underlying processes that produce that ability are not themselves simulatable computationally at some level of description.

Furthermore there is another persistent confusion in Penrose's argument over the notion of computability. He thinks that the computable character of neurons makes each neuron somehow into a little computer, the "neural computer," as he calls it. But this is another fallacy. The trajectory of a baseball is computable and can be simulated on a computer. But this does not make baseballs into little computers.

To summarize my objections to Penrose's argument in this book:

1. I do not believe he has shown that Gödel's theorem implies that Weak AI is false. Even as patched up to meet the Putnam-style objection, the argument is still fallacious.

2. Even if he had shown Weak AI to be false, it does not follow that the explanation of our noncomputable cognitive capacities would have to be given with reference to elements that are noncomputable. Neuronal behavior could still provide the explanation of consciousness.

3. From the fact that an entity such as a neuron can be simulated on a computer, it does not follow that the entity is itself a computer, a "neuronal computer."

* * * *

Penrose is so intelligent and the book contains so many dazzling passages that one has to make an effort to remind oneself of its unrealistic Alice-in-Wonderland qualities. As
Penrose must be aware, it makes no sense in the abstract
to ask, "Is consciousness computable?" It would be like asking
"Are shoes computable?" The question only makes sense relative to a specification of which features of consciousness we
are talking about and at what level of abstraction we are talking. And once that specification has been made, the answers
must be trivial. If the question asks, "Can truths which can be
consciously known but cannot be proved as theorems be
proved with a theorem proving algorithm?" the answer is trivially no. If the question asks, "Is there some level of description at which conscious processes and their correlated brain
processes can be simulated?" the answer is trivially yes.
Anything that can be described as a precise series of steps can
be simulated.

I have not explored the deeper metaphysical presuppositions behind Penrose's entire argument. He comes armed with
the credentials of science and mathematics, but he is also a
classical metaphysician, a self-declared Platonist. He believes
we live in three worlds, the physical, the mental, and the
mathematical. He wants to show how each world grounds the
next in an endless circle. The physical world grounds the mental world which in turn grounds the mathematical world and
the mathematical world is the ground of the physical world
and so on around the circle. I think it is fair to say that he does
not give a coherent account of what these grounding relations

are or how it is all supposed to work.[10] I do not think a coherent account can be given, and I want to suggest an alternative metaphysical picture that is at least consistent with what we know about how the world really works.

We live in exactly one world. I think it best to abandon the traditional Cartesian categories of "mental" and "physical" for describing that world, since it contains all kinds of things—money, interest rates, reasons for voting for or against the Democratic candidate, laws of logic, points scored in football games—that are not in any obvious sense either mental or physical. In that one world there are biological beasts like ourselves that have conscious mental states. Some of these beasts, us for example, have a language and that enables us to do things such as count, add, subtract, multiply, and divide. Because these mathematical operations are objective, we get the illusion that they give us access to another world, a world of numbers. But that is an illusion. Numbers are not part of another world, any more than the meanings of words are part of another world. They are part of our system for representing and otherwise coping with the only world there is.

We live in one world, not two or three or twenty-seven. The main task of a philosophy and science of consciousness right now is to show how consciousness is a biological part of that world, along with digestion, photosynthesis, and all the rest of it. Admiring Penrose and his work, I conclude that the

---

10. In a subsequent work, Penrose continues to defend the three-worlds conception of reality. Roger Penrose, *The Large, the Small and the Human Mind*, with Abner Shimony, Nancy Cartwright, and Stephen Hawking, edited by Malcolm Longair (Cambridge University Press, 1997).

chief value of *Shadows of the Mind* is that from it you can learn a lot about Gödel's theorem and about quantum mechanics. You will not learn much about consciousness.

Gödel's Proof and Computers

This is my own version of Penrose's version of Turing's version of Gödel's incompleteness proof, which Penrose uses to try to prove Lucas's claim. It is usually called "the proof of the unsolvability of the halting problem."

Penrose does not provide a rigorous proof, but a summary, and this is a summary of his summary. Some problems with his account are that he does not distinguish computational procedures from computational results, but assumes without argument that they are equivalent; he leaves out the quantifiers "there is an X such that" and "for every X, X is such that"; and he introduces the epistemic notions of "known" and "knowable," which are not part of the original proofs. In what follows, for greater clarity I have tried to remove some of the ambiguities in his original and I have put my own comments in parentheses.

Step 1. Some computational procedures stop (or halt). Recall our previous example: if we tell our computer to start with the numbers 1, 2, etc., and search for a number larger than 8 it will stop on 9. But some do not stop. For example, if we tell our computer to search for an odd number that is the sum of two even numbers it will never stop, because there is no such number.

Step 2. We can generalize this point. For any number n we can think of computational procedures C_1, C_2, C_3, etc., on n as dividing into two kinds, those that stop and those that do not stop. Thus the procedure: search for a number bigger than n, stops at $n + 1$ because the search is then over. The procedure: search for an odd number that is the sum of n even numbers never stops because no procedure can ever find any such number.

Step 3. Now how can we find out which procedures never stop? Well suppose we had another procedure (or finite set of procedures) A which when it stops would tell us that the procedure $C(n)$ does not stop. Think of A as the sum total of all the *knowable and sound* methods for deciding when computational procedures stop.

So if the procedure A stops then $C(n)$ does not stop.

(Penrose asks us just to assume as a premise that there are such procedures and that we know them. This is where epistemology gets in. We are to think of these procedures as knowable to us and as "sound." It is a nonstandard use of the notion of soundness to apply it to computational procedures. What he means is that such a procedure always gives true or correct results [p. 73].)

Step 4. Now think of a series of computations numbered $C_1(n)$, $C_2(n)$, $C_3(n)$, etc. These are all the computations that can be performed on n, all the possible computations. These would include multiplying a number by n, squaring n, adding n to itself, etc. And we are to think of them as numbered in some systematic way.

Step 5. But since we have now numbered all the possible computations on n we can think of A as a computational procedure which given any two numbers q and n tries to determine whether $C_q(n)$ never stops. Suppose, for example, that $q=17$ and $n=8$. Then the job for A is to figure out whether the 17th computation on 8 stops. Thus, if $A(q,n)$ stops, then $C_q(n)$ does not stop. (Notice that A operates on ordered pairs of numbers q and n, but C_1, C_2, etc., are computations on single numbers. We get around this difference in the next step.)

Step 6. Now consider cases where $q=n$. In such cases, for all n,

if $A(n,n)$ stops, then $C_n(n)$ does not stop.

Step 7. In such cases A has only one number n to worry about, the nth computation on the number n, and not two different numbers. But we said back in step 4 that the series $C_1(n)$, $C_2(n)$... included *all* the computations on n, so for any n, $A(n,n)$ has to be one member of the series $C_n(n)$. Well, suppose that $A(n,n)$ is the kth computation on n, that is, suppose

$A(n,n) = C_k(n)$

Step 8. Now examine the case of $n=k$. In such a case,

$A(k,k) = C_k(k)$

Step 9. From step 6 it follows that

if $A(k,k)$ stops, then $C_k(k)$ does not stop.

Step 10. But substituting the identity stated in step 8 we get if $C_k(k)$ stops, then $C_k(k)$ does not stop.

But if a proposition implies its own negation, it is false. Therefore:

$C_k(k)$ does not stop.

Step 11. It follows immediately that $A(k,k)$ does not stop either, because it is the same computation as $C_k(k)$. And that has the result that our known sound procedures are insufficient to tell us that $C_k(k)$ does not stop, even though in fact it does not stop, and we know that it does not stop.

But then A can't tell us what we know, namely

$C_k(k)$ does not stop.

Step 12. Thus from the knowledge that A is sound we can show that there are some nonstopping computational procedures, such as $C_k(k)$, that cannot be shown to be nonstopping by A. So we know something that A cannot tell us, so A is not sufficient to express our understanding.

Step 13. But A included all the *knowably sound* algorithms we had.

(Penrose says not just "known sound" but "knowably sound." The argument so far doesn't justify that move, but I think he would claim that the argument works not just for anything we in fact know but for anything we could know. So I have left it as he says it.)

Thus no knowably sound set of computational procedures such as A can ever be sufficient to determine that computations do not stop, because there are some such as $C_k(k)$

that they cannot capture. So we are not using a knowably sound algorithm to figure out what we know.

Step 14. So we are not computers.

Chapter Five

Consciousness Denied:
Daniel Dennett's Account

Daniel Dennett is a philosopher who has written a number of books on the philosophy of mind, but it seems clear that he regards *Consciousness Explained*[1] as the culmination of his work in this field. That work is in the tradition of behaviorism—the idea that behavior and dispositions to behavior are somehow constitutive of mental states—and verificationism—the idea that the only things which exist are those whose presence can be verified by scientific means. Though at first sight he appears to be advocating a scientific approach to consciousness comparable to those of Crick, Penrose, and Edelman, there are some very important differences, as we will see.

Before discussing his *Consciousness Explained*, I want to ask the reader to perform a small experiment to remind himself or herself of what exactly is at issue in theories of consciousness. Take your right hand and pinch the skin on your left forearm. What exactly happened when you did so? Several

1. Little, Brown, 1991.

different sorts of things happened. First, the neurobiologists tell us, the pressure of your thumb and forefinger set up a sequence of neuron firings that began at the sensory receptors in your skin, went into the spine and up the spine through a region called the tract of Lissauer, and then into the thalamus and other basal regions of the brain. The signal then went to the somato-sensory cortex and perhaps other cortical regions as well. A few hundred milliseconds after you pinched your skin, a second sort of thing happened, one that you know about without professional assistance. You felt a pain. Nothing serious, just a mildly unpleasant pinching sensation in the skin of your forearm. This unpleasant sensation had a certain particular sort of subjective feel to it, a feel which is accessible to you in a way it is not accessible to others around you. This accessibility has epistemic consequences—you can know about your pain in a way that others cannot—but the subjectivity is ontological rather than epistemic. That is, the mode of existence of the sensation is a first-person or subjective mode of existence, whereas the mode of existence of the neural pathways is a third-person or objective mode of existence; the pathways exist independently of being experienced in a way that the pain does not. The feeling of the pain is one of the "qualia" I mentioned earlier.

Furthermore, when you pinched your skin, a third sort of thing happened. You acquired a behavioral disposition you did not previously have. If someone asks you, "Did you feel anything?" you would say something like, "Yes, I felt a mild pinch right here." No doubt other things happened as well— you altered the gravitational relations between your right hand and the moon, for example—but let us concentrate on these first three.

If you were asked what is the essential thing about the sensation of pain, I think you would say that the second feature, the feeling, is the pain itself. The input signals *cause* the pain, and the pain in turn causes you to have a behavioral disposition. But the essential thing about the pain is that it is a specific internal qualitative feeling. The problem of consciousness in both philosophy and the natural sciences is to explain these subjective feelings. Not all of them are bodily sensations like pain. The stream of conscious thought is not a bodily sensation comparable to feeling pinched and neither are visual experiences, yet both have the quality of ontological subjectivity that I have been talking about. The subjective feelings are the *data* that a theory of consciousness has to explain, and the account of the neural pathways that I sketched is a partial *theory* to account for the data. The behavioral dispositions are not part of the conscious experience, but they are caused by it.

The peculiarity of Daniel Dennett's book can now be stated: he denies the existence of the data. He thinks there are no such things as the second sort of entity, the feeling of pain. He thinks there are no such things as qualia, subjective experiences, first-person phenomena, or any of the rest of it. Dennett agrees that it *seems to us* that there are such things as qualia, but this is a matter of a mistaken judgment we are making about what really happens. Well, what does really happen according to him?

What really happens, according to Dennett, is that we have stimulus inputs, such as the pressure on your skin in my experiment, and we have dispositions to behavior, "reactive dispositions" as he calls them. And in between there are "discriminative states" that cause us to respond differently to different pressures on the skin and to discriminate red from green, etc., but the sort of state that we have for discriminating pressure is exactly like the state of a machine for detecting pressure. It does not experience any special feeling; indeed it does not have any inner feelings at all, because there are no such things as "inner feelings." It is all a matter of third-person phenomena: stimulus inputs, discriminative states (p. 372 ff.), and reactive dispositions. The feature that makes these all hang together is that our brains are a type of computer and consciousness is a certain sort of software, a "virtual machine" in our brain.

The main point of Dennett's book is to deny the existence of inner mental states and offer an alternative account of consciousness, or rather what *he* calls "consciousness." The net effect is a performance of *Hamlet* without the Prince of Denmark. Dennett, however, does not begin on page one to tell us that he thinks conscious states, as I have described them, do not exist, and that there is nothing there but a brain implementing a computer program. Rather, he spends the first two hundred pages discussing questions which seem to presuppose the existence of subjective conscious states and proposing a methodology for investigating consciousness. For example, he discusses various perceptual illusions such as the so-called *phi* phenomenon. In this illusion, when two small spots in front of you are briefly lit in rapid succession it seems to you that a single spot is moving back and forth. The way we ordinarily understand such examples is in terms of our having an inner subjective experience of seeming to see a single spot moving back and forth. But that is not what Dennett has in mind. He wants to deny the existence of any inner qualia, but this does not emerge until much later in the book. He does not, in short, write with the candor of a man who is completely confident of his thesis and anxious to get it out into the open as quickly as he can. On the contrary, there is a certain evasiveness about the early chapters, since he conceals what he really thinks. It is not until after page 200 that you get his account of "consciousness," and not until well after page 350 that you find out what is really going on.

The main issue in the first part of the book is to defend what he calls the "Multiple Drafts" model of consciousness as opposed to the "Cartesian Theater" model. The idea, says Dennett, is that we are tacitly inclined to think that there must be a single place in the brain where it all comes together, a kind of Cartesian Theater where we witness the play of our consciousness. And in opposition he wants to advance the view that a whole series of information states are going on in the brain, rather like multiple drafts of an article. On the surface, this might appear to be an interesting issue for neurobiology: where in the brain are our subjective experiences localized? Is there a single locus or many? A single locus, by the way, would seem neurobiologically implausible, because any organ in the brain that might seem essential to consciousness, as for example the thalamus is essential according to Crick's hypothesis, has a twin on the other side of the brain. Each lobe has its own thalamus. But that is not what Dennett is driving at. He is attacking the Cartesian Theater not because he thinks subjective states occur all over the brain, but rather because he does not think there are any such things as subjective states at all and he wants to soften up the opposition to his counterintuitive (to put it mildly) views by first getting rid of the idea that there is a unified locus of our conscious experiences.

If Dennett denies the existence of conscious states as we usually think of them, what is his alternative account? Not surprisingly, it is a version of Strong AI. In order to explain it, I must first briefly explain four notions that he uses: von Neumann machines, connectionism, virtual machines, and memes. A digital computer, the kind you are likely to buy in a store today, proceeds by a series of steps performed very rapidly, millions per second. This is called a serial computer, and because the initial designs were by John von Neumann, a Hungarian-American scientist and mathematician, it is sometimes called a von Neumann machine. Recently there have been efforts to build machines that operate in parallel, that is, with several computational channels working at once and interacting with each other. In physical structure these are more like human brains. They are not really much like brains, but certainly they are more like brains than the traditional von Neumann machines. Computations of this type are called variously Parallel Distributed Processing, Neuronal Net Modeling, or simply Connectionism. Strictly speaking, any computation that can be performed on a connectionist structure—or "architecture," as it is usually called—can also be performed on a serial architecture, but connectionist nets have some other interesting properties: for example, they are faster and they can "learn"—that is, they can change their behavior—by having the strengths of the connections altered.

Here is how a typical connectionist net works (fig. 5). There are a series of nodes at the input level that receive inputs. These can be represented as certain numerical values, 1, -1, 1/2, etc. These values are transmitted over all of the connections to the next nodes in line at the next level. Each

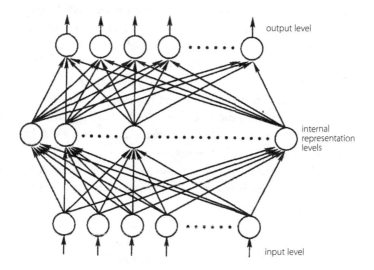

Fig. 5. A simple multilayer network. Each unit connects to all units in the layer above it. There are no sideways connections, or back connections. The "internal representation levels" are often referred to as the "hidden levels"

connection has a certain strength, and these connection strengths can also be represented as numerical values, 1, −1, 1/2, etc. The input signal is multiplied by the connection strength to get the value that is received by the next node from that connection. Thus, for example, an input of 1 multiplied by a connection strength of 1/2 gives a value of 1/2 from that connection to the next node in line. The nodes that receive these signals do a summation of all the numerical values they have received and send out those values to the next set of nodes in line. So there is an input level, an output level, and a series of one or more interior levels called "hidden levels." The series of processes continues until the output level is reached. In cognitive science, the numbers are used to represent features of some cognitive process that is being modeled, for example features of faces in face recognition, or sounds of words in a model of the pronunciation of English. The sense in which the network "learns" is that you can get the right match between the input values and the output values by fiddling with the connection strengths until you get the match you want. This is usually done by another computer, called a "teacher."

These systems are sometimes said to be "neuronally inspired." The idea is that we are to think of the connections as something like axons and dendrites, and the nodes as something like the cell bodies that do a summation of the input values and then decide how much of a signal to send to the next "neurons," i.e., the next connections and nodes in line.

Another notion Dennett uses is that of a "virtual machine." The actual machine I am now working on is made of actual wires, transistors, etc.; in addition, we can get machines like mine to simulate the structure of another type of machine. The other machine is not actually part of the wiring of this machine but exists entirely in the patterns of regularities that can be imposed on the wiring of my machine. This is called the virtual machine.

The last notion Dennett uses is that of a "meme." This notion is not very clear. It was invented by Richard Dawkins to have a cultural analog to the biological notion of a gene. The idea is that just as biological evolution occurs by way of genes, so cultural evolution occurs through the spread of memes. On Dawkins's definition, quoted by Dennett, a meme is

a unit of cultural transmission, or a unit of *imitation....*
Examples of memes are tunes, ideas, catch-phrases,
clothes, fashions, ways of making pots or of building
arches. Just as genes propagate themselves in the gene
pool by leaping from body to body via sperm or eggs, so
memes propagate themselves in the meme pool by leaping from brain to brain via a process which, in the broad
sense, can be called imitation. [p. 202]

I believe the analogy between "gene" and "meme" is
mistaken. Biological evolution proceeds by brute, blind, natural forces. The spread of ideas and theories by "imitation" is
typically a conscious process directed toward a goal. It misses
the point of Darwin's account of the origin of species to lump
the two sorts of processes together. Darwin's greatest achievement was to show that the appearance of purpose, planning,
teleology, and intentionality in the origin and development of
human and animal species was entirely an illusion. The appearance could be explained by evolutionary processes that contained no such purposes at all. But the spread of ideas through
imitation requires the whole apparatus of human consciousness and intentionality. Ideas have to be understood and inter-
preted. And they have to be understood and judged as desirable
or undesirable, in order to be treated as candidates for imitation
or rejection. Imitation typically requires a conscious effort on
the part of the imitator. The whole process normally involves
language with all its variability and subtlety. In short, the
transmission of ideas through imitation is totally unlike the
transmission of genes through reproduction, so the analogy
between genes and memes is misleading from the start.

On the basis of these four notions, Dennett offers the following explanation of consciousness:

> Human consciousness is *itself* a huge collection of memes (or more exactly, meme-effects in brains) that can best be understood as the operation of a *"von Neumannesque"* virtual machine *implemented* in the *parallel architecture* of a brain that was not designed for any such activities. [italics in the original, p. 210]

In other words, being conscious is entirely a matter of implementing a certain sort of computer program or programs in a parallel machine that evolved in nature.

It is essential to see that once Dennett has denied the existence of conscious states he does not see any need for additional arguments to get to Strong AI. All of the moves in the conjuring trick have already been made. Strong AI seems to him the only reasonable way to account for a machine that lacks any qualitative, subjective, inner mental contents but behaves in complex ways. The extreme anti-mentalism of his views has been missed by several of Dennett's critics, who have pointed out that, according to his theory, he cannot distinguish between human beings and unconscious zombies who behaved exactly as if they were human beings. Dennett's riposte is to say that there could not be any such zombies, that any machine regardless of what it is made of that behaved like us would have to have consciousness just as we do. This looks as if he is claiming that sufficiently complex zombies would not be zombies but would have inner conscious states the same as ours; but that is emphatically not the claim he is making. His claim is that in fact *we are zombies*, that there is no difference between us and machines that lack conscious states in the sense I have explained. The claim is not that the sufficiently complex zombie would suddenly come to conscious life, just as Galatea was brought to life by Pygmalion. Rather, Dennett argues that there is no such thing as conscious life, for us, for animals, for zombies, or for anything else; there is only complex zombiehood. In one of his several discussions of zombies, he considers whether there is any difference between human pain and suffering and a zombie's pain and suffering. This is in a section about pain where the idea is that pain is not the name of a sensation but rather a matter of having one's plans thwarted and one's hopes crushed, and the idea is that the zombie's "suffering" is no different from our conscious suffering:

> Why should a "zombie's" crushed hopes matter less than a conscious person's crushed hopes? There is a trick with mirrors here that should be exposed and discarded. Consciousness, you say, is what matters, but then you cling to doctrines about consciousness that systematically prevent us from getting any purchase on why it matters. Postulating special inner qualities that are not only private and intrinsically valuable, but also unconfirmable and uninvestigatable is just obscurantism. [p. 450]

The rhetorical flourishes here are typical of the book, but to bring the discussion down to earth, ask yourself, when you performed the experiment of pinching yourself were you "postulating special inner qualities" that are "unconfirmable and uninvestigatable"? Were you being "obscurantist"? And most important, is there no difference at all between you who have pains and an unconscious zombie that behaves like you but has no pains or any other conscious states?

Actually, though the question with which Dennett's passage begins is intended to be as rhetorical as the ones I just asked, it in fact has a rather easy correct answer, which Dennett did not intend. The reason a zombie's "crushed hopes" matter less than a conscious person's crushed hopes is that zombies, by definition, have no feelings whatever. Consequently nothing literally matters about their inner feelings, because they do not have any. They just have external behavior which is like the behavior of people who do have feelings and for whom things literally do matter.

Since Dennett defends a version of Strong AI it is not surprising that he takes up the Chinese Room Argument, summarized earlier, which presents the hypothesis of a man in a room who does not know Chinese but nevertheless is carrying out the steps in a program to give a simulation of a Chinese speaker. This time the objection to it is that the man in the room really could not in fact convincingly carry out the steps. The answer to this is to say that of course we could not do this in real life. The reason we have thought experiments is because for many ideas we wish to test, it is impossible to carry out the experiment in reality. In Einstein's famous discussion of the clock paradox he asks us to imagine that we go to the nearest star in a rocket ship that travels at 90 percent of the speed of light. It really does miss the point totally—though it is quite true—to say that we could not in practice build such a rocket ship.

Similarly it misses the point of the Chinese Room

thought experiment to say that we could not in practice design a program complex enough to fool native Chinese speakers but simple enough that an English speaker could carry it out in real time. In fact we cannot even design programs for commercial computers that can fool an able speaker of any natural language, but that is beside the point. The point of the Chinese Room Argument, as I hope I made clear, is to remind us that the syntax of the program is not sufficient for the semantic content (or mental content or meaning) in the mind of the Chinese speaker. Now why does Dennett not face the actual argument as I have stated it? Why does he not address that point? Why does he not tell us which of the three premises in the Chinese Room Argument he rejects? They are not very complicated and take the following form: (1) programs are syntactical, (2) minds have semantic contents, (3) syntax by itself is not the same as nor sufficient for semantic content. I think the answer is clear. He does not address the actual formal argument because to do so he would have to admit that what he really objects to is premise (2), the claim that minds have mental contents.[2] Given his assumptions, he is forced to deny that minds really do have *intrinsic* mental contents. Most people who defend Strong AI think that the computer might have mental contents just as we do, and they mistakenly take Dennett as an ally. But he does not think that computers have mental contents, because he does not think there are any such

---

2. In his response to the publication of the original article on which this chapter is based, Dennett pointed out that in other writings he had rejected *all three* premises. This response together with my rejoinder is printed as an appendix to this chapter. I believe the issues are adequately clarified in my rejoinder to Dennett.

things. For Dennett, we and the computer are both in the same situation as far as the mind is concerned, not because the computer can acquire the sorts of intrinsic mental contents that any normal human has, but because there never were any such things as intrinsic mental contents to start with.

At this point we can make clear some of the differences between Dennett's approach to consciousness and the approach I advocate, an approach which, if I understand them correctly, is also advocated by some of the other authors under discussion, including Crick, Penrose, Edelman, and Rosenfield. I believe that the brain *causes* conscious experiences. These are inner, qualitative, subjective states. In principle at least it might be possible to build an artifact, an artificial brain, that also would cause these inner states. For all we know we might build such a system using a chemistry totally different from that of the brain. We just do not know enough now about how the brain does it to know how to build an artificial system that would have causal powers equivalent to the brain's using some different mechanisms. But we do know that any other system capable of causing consciousness would have to have causal powers equivalent to the brain's to do it. This point follows trivially from the fact that brains do it causally. But there is not and cannot be any question whether a machine can be conscious and can think, because the brain is a machine. Furthermore, as I pointed out earlier, there is no known obstacle in principle to building an artificial machine that can be conscious and can think.

Now, as a purely verbal point, since we can describe any system under some computational description or other, we might even describe our artificial conscious machine as a "computer" and this might make it look as if the position I am advocating is consistent with Dennett's. But in fact the two approaches are radically different. Dennett does not believe that the brain causes inner qualitative conscious states, because he does not believe that there are any such things. On my view the computational aspects of an artificial conscious machine would be something *in addition* to consciousness. On Dennett's view there is no consciousness in addition to the computational features, because that is all that consciousness amounts to for him: meme effects of a von Neumann(esque) virtual machine implemented in a parallel architecture.

Dennett's book is unique among the several books under discussion here in that it makes no contribution to the problem of consciousness but rather denies that there is any such problem in the first place. Dennett, as Kierkegaard said in another connection, keeps the forms, while stripping them of their significance. He keeps the vocabulary of consciousness, while denying its existence.

But someone might object: Is it not possible that science might discover that Dennett was right, that there really are no such things as inner qualitative mental states, that the whole thing is an illusion like sunsets? After all, if science can discover that sunsets are a systematic illusion, why could it not also discover that conscious states such as pains are illusions too? There is this difference: in the case of sunsets science does not deny the existence of the datum, that the sun appears to move through the sky. Rather it gives an alternative explanation of this and other data. Science preserves the appearance while giving us a deeper insight into the reality behind the appearance. But Dennett denies the existence of the data to start with.

But couldn't we disprove the existence of these data by proving that they are only illusions? No, you can't disprove the existence of conscious experiences by proving that they are only an appearance disguising the underlying reality, because *where consciousness is concerned the existence of the appearance is the reality.* If it seems to me exactly as if I am having conscious experiences, then I am having conscious experiences. This is not an epistemic point. I might make various sorts of mistakes about my experiences, for example, if I suffered from phantom limb pains. But whether reliably reported or not, the experience of feeling the pain is identical with the pain in a way that the experience of seeing a sunset is not identical with a sunset.

I regard Dennett's denial of the existence of consciousness not as a new discovery or even as a serious possibility but rather as a form of intellectual pathology. The interest of his account lies in figuring out what assumptions could lead an intelligent person to paint himself into such a corner. In Dennett's case the answers are not hard to find. He tells us: "The idea at its simplest was that since you can never 'see directly' into people's minds, but have to take their word for it, any such facts as there are about mental events are not among the data of science" (pp. 70–71). And later,

> Even if mental events are not among the *data* of science, this does not mean we cannot study them scientifically.... The challenge is to construct a theory of mental events, using the data that scientific method permits. Such a theory will have to be constructed from the

third-person point of view, since *all* science is constructed from that perspective. [p. 71]

Scientific objectivity according to Dennett's conception
requires the "third-person point of view." At the end of his
book he combines this view with verificationism—the idea
that only things that can be scientifically verified really exist.
These two theories lead him to deny that there can exist any
phenomena that have a first-person ontology. That is, his
denial of the existence of consciousness derives from two
premises: scientific verification always takes the third-person
point of view, and nothing exists which cannot be verified by
scientific verification so construed. This is the deepest mistake
in the book and it is the source of most of the others, so I want
to end this discussion by exposing it.

We need to distinguish the *epistemic* sense of the distinction between the first- and the third-person points of view,
(i.e., between the subjective and the objective) from the *ontological* sense. Some statements can be known to be true or false
independently of any prejudices or attitudes on the part of
observers. They are objective in the epistemic sense. For example, if I say, "Van Gogh died in Auvers-sur-Oise, France," that
statement is epistemically objective. Its truth has nothing to
do with anyone's personal prejudices or preferences. But if I
say, for example, "Van Gogh was a better painter than Renoir,"
that statement is epistemically subjective. Its truth or falsity
is a matter at least in part of the attitudes and preferences of
observers. In addition to this sense of the objective–subjective
distinction, there is an ontological sense. Some entities,
mountains for example, have an existence which is objective

in the sense that it does not depend on any subject. Others, pain for example, are subjective in that their existence depends on being felt by a subject. They have a first-person or subjective ontology.

Now here is the point. Science does indeed aim at epistemic objectivity. The aim is to get a set of truths that are free of our special preferences and prejudices. But epistemic objectivity of *method* does not require ontological objectivity of *subject matter*. It is just an objective fact—in the epistemic sense—that I and people like me have pains. But the mode of existence of these pains is subjective—in the ontological sense. Dennett has a definition of science which excludes the possibility that science might investigate subjectivity, and he thinks the third-person objectivity of science forces him to this definition. But that is a bad pun on "objectivity." The aim of science is to get a systematic account of how the world works. One part of the world consists of ontologically subjective phenomena. If we have a definition of science that forbids us from investigating that part of the world, it is the definition that has to be changed and not the world.

I do not wish to give the impression that all 511 pages of Dennett's book consist in repeating the same mistake over and over. On the contrary, he makes many valuable points and is especially good at summarizing much of the current work in neurobiology and cognitive science. For example, he provides an interesting discussion of the complex relations between the temporal order of events in the world that the brain represents and the temporal order of the representing that goes on in the brain.

Dennett's prose, as some reviewers have pointed out, is breezy and sometimes funny, but at crucial points it is imprecise and evasive, as I have tried to explain here. At his worst he tries to bully the reader with abusive language and rhetorical questions, as the passage about zombies above illustrates. A typical move is to describe the opposing view as relying on "ineffable" entities. But there is nothing ineffable about the pain you feel when you pinch yourself.

An Exchange with Daniel Dennett

Following publication of the original article on which this chapter is based, Daniel Dennett and I had the following exchange in The New York Review of Books.

DANIEL DENNETT writes:

John Searle and I have a deep disagreement about how to study the mind. For Searle, it is all really quite simple. There are these bedrock, time-tested intuitions we all have about consciousness, and any theory that challenges them is just preposterous. I, on the contrary, think that the persistent problem of consciousness is going to remain a mystery until we find some such dead obvious intuition and show that, in spite of first appearances, it is false! One of us is dead wrong, and the stakes are high. Searle sees my position as "a form of intellectual pathology"; no one should be surprised to learn that the feeling is mutual. Searle has tradition on his side. My view is remarkably counterintuitive at first, as he says. But his view has some problems, too, which emerge only after some rather subtle analysis. Now how do we proceed? We each try to mount arguments to demonstrate our case and show the other side is wrong.

For my part, knowing that I had to move a huge weight of traditional opinion, I tried something indirect: I deliberately postponed addressing the big fat philosophical questions until I could build up quite an elaborate theory on which to found an alternative perspective—only then did I try to show the readers how they could live with its counterintuitive implications after all. Searle doesn't like this strategy of mine; he accuses me of lack of candor and detects "a certain evasiveness" about the early chapters, since "he conceals what he really thinks." Nonsense. I went out of my way at the beginning to address this very issue (my little parable of the madman who says there are no animals, pp. 43–45), warning the reader of what was to come. No cards up my sleeve, but watch out—I'm coming after some of your most deeply cherished intuitions.

For his part, he has one argument, the Chinese Room, and he has been trotting it out, basically unchanged, for fifteen years. It has proven to be an amazingly popular number among the non-experts, in spite of the fact that just about everyone who knows anything about the field dismissed it long ago. It is full of well-concealed fallacies. By Searle's own count, there are over a hundred published attacks on it. He can count them, but I guess he can't read them, for in all those years he has never to my knowledge responded in detail to the dozens of devastating criticisms they contain; he has just presented the basic thought experiment over and over again. I just went back and counted: I am dismayed to discover that no less than seven of those published criticisms are by me (in 1980, 1982, 1984, 1985, 1987, 1990, 1991, 1993). Searle debated me furiously in the pages of *The New York Review of Books* back in 1982, when Douglas Hofstadter and I first exposed the cute tricks that make the Chinese Room "work." That was the last time Searle addressed any of my specific criticisms until now. Now he trots out the Chinese Room yet one more time and has the audacity to ask "Now why does Dennett not face the actual argument as I have stated it? Why does he not tell us which of the three premises he rejects in the Chinese Room Argument?" Well, because I have already done so, in great detail, in several of the articles he has never deigned to answer. For instance, in "Fast Thinking" (way back in *The Intentional Stance*, 1987) I explicitly quoted his entire three-premise argument and showed exactly why *all three of them* are false, when given the interpretation they need for the argument to go through! Why didn't I repeat that 1987 article in my 1991 book? Because, unlike Searle, I had gone on to other things. I did, however, cite my 1987 article prominently in a footnote (p. 436), and noted that Searle's only response to it had been simply to declare, without argument, that the points offered there were irrelevant. The pattern continues; now he both ignores that challenge and goes on to misrepresent the further criticisms of the Chinese Room that I offered in the book under review, but perhaps he has forgotten what I actually wrote in the four years it has taken him to write his review.

But enough about the Chinese Room. What do I have to offer on my side? I have my candidate for the fatally false intuition, and it is indeed the very intuition Searle invites the reader to share with him, the conviction that we know what we're talking about when we talk about *that feeling*—you know, the feeling of pain that is the effect of the stimulus and the cause of the dispositions to react—the *quale*, the "intrinsic" content of the subjective state. How could anyone deny that!? Just watch—but you have to pay close attention. I develop my destructive arguments against this intuition by showing how an objective science of consciousness is possible after all, and how Searle's proposed "first-person" alternative leads to self-contradiction and paradox at every turning. This is the "deepest mistake" in my book, according to Searle, and he sets out to "expose" it. The trouble is that the objective scientific method I describe (under the alarming name of heterophenomenology) is nothing I invented; it is in fact exactly the method tacitly endorsed and relied upon by every scientist working on consciousness, including Crick, Edelman, and Rosenfield. They have no truck with Searle's "intrinsic" content and "ontological subjectivity"; they know better.

Searle brings this out amusingly in his own essay. He heaps praise on Gerald Edelman's neuroscientific theory of consciousness, but points out at the end that it has a minor problem—it isn't about consciousness! "So the mystery remains." Edelman's theory is not about Searle's brand of consciousness, that's for sure. No scientific theory could be. But Edelman's theory *is* about consciousness, and has some good points to make. (The points of Edelman's that Searle admiringly recounts are not really the original part of Edelman's theory—they are more or less taken for granted by everyone working on the topic, though Edelman is right to emphasize them. If Searle had read me in the field he would realize that.) Edelman supports his theory with computer simulations such as Darwin III, which Searle carefully describes as "Weak AI." But in fact Edelman has insisted to me, correctly, that his robot exhibits intentionality as real as any on the planet—it's just artificial intentionality, and none the worse for that. Edelman got off on the wrong foot by buying Searle's Chinese Room for a while, but by now I think he's seen the light. GOFAI (Good Old-Fashioned AI—the agent-as-walking-encyclopedia) is dead, but Strong AI is not dead; computational neuroscience is a brand of it. Crick's doing it; Edelman's doing it; the Churchlands are doing it, I'm doing it, and so are hundreds of others.

Not Searle. Searle doesn't have a program of research. He has a set of home truths to defend. They land him in paradox after paradox, but so long as he doesn't address the critics who point this out, who'll ever know? For a detailed analysis of the embarrassments in Searle's position, see my review of *The Rediscovery of the Mind*, in *Journal of Philosophy*, Vol. 60, No. 4, April 1993, pp. 193–205. It recounts case after case of Searle ignoring or misrepresenting his critics, and invites him to dispel the strong impression that this has been deliberate on his part. Searle's essay in these pages is his only response to that invitation, confirming once again the pattern, as readers familiar with the literature will realize. There is not room in these pages for Searle to repair fifteen years of disregard, so no one should expect him to make good here, but if he would be so kind as to tell us where and when he intends to respond to his critics with the attention and accuracy they deserve, we will know when to resume paying attention to his claims.

JOHN SEARLE replies:

In spite of its strident tone, I am grateful for Daniel Dennett's response to my review because it enables me to make the differences between us crystal clear. I think we all really have conscious states. To remind everyone of this fact I asked my readers to perform the small experiment of pinching the left forearm with the right hand to produce a small pain. The pain has a certain sort of qualitative feeling to it, and such qualitative feelings are typical of the various sorts of conscious events that form the content of our waking and dreaming lives. To make explicit the differences between conscious events and, for example, mountains and molecules, I said consciousness has a first-person or subjective ontology. By that I mean that conscious states only exist when experienced by a subject and they exist only from the first-person point of view of that subject.

Such events are the data which a theory of consciousness is supposed to explain. In my account of consciousness I start with the data; Dennett denies the existence of the data. To put it as clearly as I can: in his book, *Consciousness Explained*, Dennett denies the existence of consciousness. He continues to use the word, but he means something different by it. For him, it refers only to third-person phenomena, not to the first-person conscious feelings and experiences we all have. For Dennett there is no difference between us humans and complex zombies who lack any inner feelings, because we are all just complex zombies.

I think most readers, when first told this, would assume that I must be misunderstanding him. Surely no sane person could deny the existence of feelings. But in his reply he makes it clear that I have understood him exactly. He says, "How could anyone deny that!? Just watch...."

I regard his view as self-refuting because it denies the existence of the data which a theory of consciousness is supposed to explain. How does he think he can, so to speak, get away with this? At this point in the argument his letter misrepresents the nature of the issues. He writes that the disagreement between us is about rival "intuitions," that it is between my "time-tested intuitions" defending "traditional opinion" against his more up-to-date intuitions, and that he and I "have a deep disagreement about how to study the mind." But the disagreement is not about intuitions and it is not about how to study the mind. It is not about methodology. It is about the existence of the object of study in the first place. An intuition in his sense is just something one feels inclined to believe, and such intuitions often turn out to be false. For example, people have intuitions about space and time that have been refuted by relativity theory in physics. In my review, I gave an example of an intuition about consciousness that has been refuted by neurobiology: the common-sense intuition that our pain in the arm is actually located in the physical space of the arm.[3] But the very existence of my conscious states is not similarly a matter for my intuitions. The refutable intuitions I mentioned require a distinction between how things seem to me and how they really are, a distinction between appearance and reality. But where the existence of conscious states is concerned, you can't make the distinction between appearance and reality, *because the existence of the*

---

3. In a section published in this book as chapter 7.

appearance is the reality in question. If it consciously seems to me that I am conscious, then I am conscious. It is not a matter of "intuitions," of something I feel inclined to say. Nor is it a matter of methodology. Rather it is just a plain fact about me—and every other normal human being—that we have sensations and other sorts of conscious states.

Now what am I to do, as a reviewer, in the face of what appears to be an obvious and self-refuting falsehood? Should I pinch the author to remind him that he is conscious? Or should I pinch myself and report the results in more detail? The method I adopted in my review was to try to diagnose what philosophical assumptions lead Dennett to deny the existence of conscious states, and as far as I can tell from his letter he has no objection to my diagnosis. He thinks the conclusion that there are no conscious states follows from two axioms that he holds explicitly, the objectivity of science and verificationism. These are, first, that science uses objective or third-person methods, and second, that nothing exists which cannot be verified by scientific methods so construed. I argued at some length in my review that the objectivity of science does not have the consequence he thinks it does. The epistemic objectivity of method does not preclude ontological subjectivity of subject matter. To state this in less fancy jargon: the fact that many people have back pains, for example, is an objective fact of medical science. The existence of these pains is not a matter of anyone's opinions or attitudes. But the mode of existence of the pains themselves is subjective. They exist only as felt by human subjects. In short the only formal argument I can find in his book for the denial of consciousness rests on a fallacy. He says nothing in his letter to respond to my argument.

But how then does he hope to defend his view? The central claim in his reply is this sentence:

> I develop my destructive arguments against this intuition by showing how an objective science of consciousness is possible after all, and how Searle's proposed "first-person" alternative leads to self-contradiction and paradox at every turning.

He makes two points: one about "objective science" and the other about "self-contradiction and paradox," so let's consider these in turn. Dennett reflects in his letter exactly the confusion about objectivity I exposed in his book. He thinks the objective methods of science make it impossible to study people's subjective feelings and experiences. This is a mistake, as should be clear from any textbook of neurology. The authors use the objective methods of science to try to explain, and help their students to cure, the inner subjective pains, anxieties, and other sufferings of their patients. There is no reason why an objective science cannot study subjective experiences. Dennett's "objective science of consciousness" changes the subject. It is not about consciousness, but rather is a third-person account of external behavior.

What about his claim that my view that we are conscious "leads to self-contradiction and paradox at every turning." The claim that he can show self-contradictions in my views, or even one self-contradiction, is, I fear, just bluff. If he can actually show or derive a formal contradiction, where is it? In the absence of any examples, the charge of self-contradiction is empty.

What about the paradoxes of consciousness? In his book he describes various puzzling and paradoxical cases from the psychological and neurobiological literature. I think these are the best parts of his book. Indeed one of the features that makes neurobiology fascinating is the existence of so many experiments with surprising and sometimes paradoxical results. The logical form of Dennett's argument is this: the paradoxical cases would not seem paradoxical if only we would give up our "intuition" that we are really conscious. But this conclusion is unwarranted. The cases are interesting to us because we all know in advance that we are conscious. Nothing in any of those experiments, paradoxical as they may be, shows that we do not have qualitative conscious states of the sort I describe. These sorts of arguments could not disprove the existence of the data, for reasons I tried to explain in my review, which I have repeated here and which Dennett does not attempt to answer. To summarize, I have claimed:

1. Dennett denies the existence of consciousness.

2. He is mistaken in thinking that the issue about the existence of consciousness is a matter of rival intuitions.

3. The philosophical argument that underlies his view is fallacious. It is a fallacy to infer from the fact that science is objective, the conclusion that it cannot recognize the existence of subjective states of consciousness.

4. The actual arguments presented in his book, which show that conscious states are often paradoxical, do not show that they do not exist.

5. The distinction between appearance and reality, which arguments like his appeal to, does not apply to the very existence of conscious states, because in such cases the appearance is the reality.

Those are the chief points I want to make. The reader in a hurry can stop here. But Dennett claims, correctly, that I don't always answer every time every accusation he makes against me. So let me take up every substantive point in his letter.

1. He claims that Crick, Edelman, and Rosenfield agree with him that conscious states as I have described them do not exist. "They have no truck" with them, he tells us. He also claims that Crick and Edelman are adherents of Strong AI. From my knowledge of these authors and their work, I have to say I found nothing in their writing to suggest they wish to deny the existence of consciousness, nothing to support the view that they adhere to Strong AI, and plenty to suggest that they disagree with Dennett on these points. Personal communication with Edelman and Crick since the publication of my review confirms my understanding of their views. Dennett cites no textual evidence to support his claims.

Indeed, Dennett is the only one of the authors I reviewed who denies the existence of the conscious experiences we are trying to explain and is the only one who thinks that all the experiences we take to be conscious are merely operations of a computing machine. In the history of the subject, however, he is by no means unique; nor is his approach new. His views are a mixture of Strong AI and an extension of the traditional behaviorism of Gilbert Ryle, Dennett's teacher in Oxford decades ago. Dennett concedes that GOFAI, Good Old-Fashioned AI, is dead. (He used to believe it. Too bad he didn't tell us why it is dead or who killed it off.) But he thinks that contemporary computational neuroscience is a form of Strong AI, and here, in my view, he is also mistaken. There are indeed experts on computational neuroscience who believe in Strong AI, but it is by no means essential to constructing computational models of neurobiological phenomena that you believe that all there is to having a mind is having the right computer program.

2. One of Dennett's claims in his letter is so transparently false as to be astonishing. He says I have ignored and not responded to criticisms of my Chinese Room Argument and to other related arguments. "Fifteen years of disregard," he tells us. This is a distinctly odd claim for someone to make in responding to a review in which I had just answered the objections he makes in his book. And it is contradicted by the record of literally dozens of occasions where I have responded to criticism. I list some of these below.[4] Much else could be cited. I have

---

4. In 1980, I responded to twenty-eight critics of the Chinese Room Argument in *Behavioral and Brain Sciences*, including Dennett, by the way. Responses to another half-dozen critics appeared in *BBS* in 1982. Still further replies to Dennett and Douglas Hofstadter appeared in these pages [of the *NYRB*] in 1982. I took up the issue again in my Reith Lectures on the BBC in 1984, published in my book, *Minds, Brains and Science*. I also debated several well-known advocates of Strong AI at the New York Academy of Science in 1984, and this was published in the academy proceedings. Another exchange in *The New York Review of Books* in 1989 with Elhanan Motzkin was followed by a debate with Paul and Patricia Churchland in *Scientific American* in 1990. There is a further published debate with Jerry Fodor in 1991 (see my response to Fodor, "Yin and Yang Strike Out" in *The Nature of Mind*, edited by David M. Rosenthal, Oxford University Press, 1991). All of this is only the material published up to the Nineties. On the tenth anniversary of the original publication, at the *BBS* editor's invitation, I published another article expanding the discussion to cognitive science explanations generally. In the ensuing debate in that journal I responded to over forty critics. More recently, in 1994 and 1995, I have responded to a series of discussions of *The Rediscovery of the Mind* in the journal *Philosophy and Phenomenological Research*. There is besides a rather hefty volume, called *John Searle and His Critics* (edited by Ernest Lepore and Robert van Gulick, Blackwell, 1991), in which I respond to many critics and commentators on all sorts of related questions.

not responded to every single objection to my views because not every objection has seemed worth responding to, but it should be clear from the record that Dennett's claim that I have not replied to criticism is simply baffling.

In recent years the issues have escalated in interesting ways. I took up the general issue of computational theories of cognition in my Presidential Address to the American Philosophical Association in 1990, and this appeared in an expanded version in my book *The Rediscovery of Mind* (1992). There I developed the argument that I restated in my review of Dennett to the effect that the Chinese Room Argument if anything conceded too much to computationalism. The original argument showed that the semantics of human cognition is not intrinsic to the formal syntactical program of a computer. My new argument shows that the syntax of the program is not intrinsic to the physics of the hardware, but rather requires an outside interpreter who assigns a computational interpretation to the system. (If I am right about this, it is devastating to Dennett's claim that we can just discover that consciousness, even in his sense, is a von Neumann machine, virtual or otherwise. In his letter, Dennett says nothing in response.)

3. Dennett's letter has a peculiar rhetorical quality in that he is constantly referring to some devastating argument against me that he never actually states. The crushing argument is always just offstage, in some review he or somebody else wrote or some book he published years ago, but he can't quite be bothered to state the argument now. When I go back and look at the arguments he refers to, I don't find them very impressive. Since he thinks they are decisive, let me mention at least one, his 1987 attack on the Chinese Room Argument.

He says correctly that when I wrote my review I took his book to be his definitive statement of his position on the Chinese Room and did not consult his earlier works. (In fact I did not know that he had produced a total of seven published attacks on this one short argument of mine until I saw his letter.) He now claims to have refuted all three premises of the argument in 1987. But I have just reread the relevant chapter of his book and find he did nothing of the sort, nor did he even make a serious effort to attack the premises. Rather he misstates my position as being about consciousness rather than about semantics. He thinks that I am only concerned to show that the man in the Chinese Room does not consciously understand Chinese, but I am in fact showing that he does not understand Chinese at all, because the syntax of the program is not sufficient for the understanding of the semantics of a language, whether conscious or unconscious. Furthermore he presupposes a kind of behaviorism. He assumes that a system that behaves as if it had mental states, must have mental states. But that kind of behaviorism is precisely what is challenged by the argument. So I have to confess that I don't find that the weakness of his arguments in his recent book is helped by his 1987 arguments.

4. Dennett resents the fact that I characterize his rhetorical style as "having a certain evasiveness" because he does not state his denial of the existence of conscious states clearly and unambiguously at the beginning of his book and then argue for it. He must have forgotten what he admitted in response to another critic who made a similar complaint, the psychologist Bruce Mangan. Here is what he said:

He [Mangan] accuses me of deliberately concealing my philosophical conclusions until late in the book, of creating a "presumptive mood," of relying on "rhetorical devices" rather than stating my "anti-realist" positions at the outset and arguing for them. Exactly! That was my strategy.... Had I opened with a frank declaration of my final conclusions I would simply have provoked a chorus of ill-concealed outrage and that brouhaha would have postponed indefinitely any remotely even-handed exploration of the position I want to defend.

What he boasts of in response to Mangan is precisely the "evasiveness" I was talking about. When Mangan makes the charge, he says, "Exactly!" When I make the same charge, he says, "Nonsense." But when a philosopher holds a view that he is pretty sure is right but which may not be popular, he should, I suggest, try to state it as clearly as he can and argue for it as strongly as he can. A "brouhaha" is not an excessive price to pay for candor.

5. Dennett says I propose no research program. That is not true. The main point of my review was to urge that we need a neurobiological account of exactly how microlevel brain processes *cause* qualitative states of consciousness, and how exactly those states are *features* of neurobiological systems. Dennett's approach would make it impossible to attack and solve these questions, which as I said, I regard as the most important questions in the biological sciences.

6. Dennett says that I advance only one argument, the Chinese Room. This is not true. There are in fact two independent sets of arguments, one about Strong AI, one about the existence of consciousness. The Chinese Room is one

argument in the first set, but the deeper argument against computationalism is that the computational features of a system are not intrinsic to its physics alone, but require a user or interpreter. Some people have made interesting criticisms of this second argument, but not Dennett in his book or in this exchange. He simply ignores it. About consciousness, I must say that if someone persistently denies the existence of consciousness itself, traditional arguments, with premises and conclusions, may never convince him. All I can do is remind the readers of the facts of their own experiences. Here is the paradox of this exchange: I am a conscious reviewer consciously answering the objections of an author who gives every indication of being consciously and puzzlingly angry. I do this for a readership that I assume is conscious. How then can I take seriously his claim that consciousness does not really exist?

POSTSCRIPT:

After the publication of this exchange, Dennett continued the discussion in other writings. Unfortunately he has a persistent problem in quoting my views accurately. Several years ago, he and his co-editor, Douglas Hofstadter, produced a volume in which they misquoted me five times.[5] I pointed this out in *The New York Review of Books*.[6] More recently, after the publication of this exchange, Dennett produced the following:

---

5. *The Mind's I: Fantasies and Reflections on Self and Soul* (BasicBooks, 1981).
6. "The Myth of the Computer," *The New York Review of Books*, April 29, 1982.

Searle is not even in the same discussion. He claims that organic brains are required to "produce" consciousness—at one point he actually said brains "secrete" consciousness, as if it were some sort of magical goo—...[7]

In the same book, he writes:

One thing we're sure about, though, is that John Searle's idea that what you call "biological material" is a necessity for agency (or consciousness) is a nonstarter. [p. 187]

The problem with both of these attributions is that they are misrepresentations and misquotations of my views. I have never maintained that "organic brains are required" to produce consciousness. We do know that certain brain functions are *sufficient* for consciousness, but we have no way of knowing at present whether they are also *necessary*. And I have never maintained the absurd view that "brains 'secrete' consciousness." It is no surprise that Dennett gives no sources for these quotations because there are none.

---

7. *Conversations in the Cognitive Neurosciences,* edited by Michael Gazzaniga (MIT Press, 1997), p. 193.

Chapter Six

David Chalmers and
the Conscious Mind

1.

Traditionally in the philosophy of mind there is supposed to be a basic distinction between dualists, who think there are two fundamentally different kinds of phenomena in the world, minds and bodies, and monists, who think that the world is made of only one kind of stuff. Dualists divide into "substance dualists," who think that "mind" and "body" name two kinds of substances, and "property dualists," who think "mental" and "physical" name different kinds of properties or features in a way that enables the same substance—a human being, for example—to have both kinds of properties at once. Monists in turn divide into idealists, who think everything is ultimately mental, and materialists, who think everything is ultimately physical or material.

I suppose most people in our civilization accept some kind of dualism. They think they have both a mind and a body, or a soul and a body. But that is emphatically not the current view among the professionals in philosophy, psychology, artificial intelligence, neurobiology, and cognitive science. Most of the people who work in these fields accept some version of materialism, because they believe that it is the only philosophy consistent with our contemporary scientific worldview. There are a few property dualists, such as Thomas Nagel and Colin McGinn, but the only substance dualists I know of are those who have a religious commitment to the existence of a soul, such as the late Sir John Eccles.

But materialists have a problem: once you have described all the material facts in the world, you still seem to have a lot of mental phenomena left over. Once you have described the facts about my body and my brain, for example, you still seem to have a lot of facts left over about my beliefs, desires, pains, etc. Materialists typically think they have to get rid of these mental facts by reducing them to material phenomena or by showing that they don't really exist at all. The history of the philosophy of mind over the past one hundred years has been in large part an attempt to get rid of the mental by showing that no mental phenomena exist over and above physical phenomena.

It is a fascinating study to try to trace these efforts, because typically their motives are hidden. The materialist philosopher purports to offer an analysis of the mental, but his or her hidden agenda is to get rid of the mental. The aim is to describe the world in materialist terms without saying anything about the mind that does not sound obviously false. That is not an easy thing to do. It sounds too implausible to say right out that pains and beliefs and desires don't exist, though some philosophers have said that. The more common materialist move is to say, yes, mental states really do exist, but they are not something in addition to physical phenomena; rather they can be reduced to, and are forms of, physical states.

The first of the great twentieth-century efforts to offer a materialist reduction of the mind was behaviorism—the view, presented by Gilbert Ryle and Carl Gustav Hempel, that mental states are just patterns of behavior and dispositions to behavior, when "behavior" just means bodily movements which have no accompanying mental component. Speech behavior, for example, according to the behaviorists' conception, is just a matter of noises coming out of one's mouth. Behaviorism sounds obviously false because, for example, everyone knows that a feeling of pain is one thing and the behavior associated with pain is another. As C. K. Ogden and I. A. Richards once remarked, to believe in behaviorism you have to be "affecting general anæsthesia."[1]

Another difficulty with behaviorism is that it is unable to account for our intuition that mental states *cause* behavior. For example, according to the behaviorist analysis, my belief that it is raining consists of patterns of behavior and dispositions to behavior. That I have such a belief consists in such facts as, for example, the fact that I wear a raincoat and carry an umbrella when I go out. (And remember, these behaviors are just bodily movements. We are not to think of them as having some mental component.) But our natural inclination is to say that the belief *causes* the behavior, not that the belief just *is* the behavior.

---

1. *The Meaning of Meaning* (Harcourt Brace, 1923), p. 23.

Furthermore, it seems the behaviorist analysis as it stands cannot be right as a reduction of the mental to behavior, because it is circular. To analyze some mental states you have to presuppose other mental states. For example, my belief that it is raining will be manifested in carrying an umbrella only if I also have a desire not to get wet. My desire not to get wet will manifest itself in this behavior only if I have the belief that the umbrella will keep me dry. So there are at least two difficulties with behaviorism besides the obvious one that it seems implausible. The first is that it cannot account for the causal relations between mind and behavior, and the second is that the relation between a mental state and behavior cannot be analyzed without mentioning other mental states. To analyze beliefs you have to have desires, and, conversely, to analyze desires you have to have beliefs.

In light of these difficulties, the next great move of the materialists was to say that mental states are identical with states of the brain. This theory, put forth by J. J. C. Smart and others, is called "physicalism" or the "identity theory," and it comes in different versions. But it too has difficulties. One difficulty is that we need to be able to explain what it is about a state of a brain that makes it a mental state as opposed to other states of the brain that are not mental states. Furthermore, it seems too restrictive to say that only brains can have mental states. Why couldn't we build a machine, for example a computer, that also had mental states but did not have anything like the physical states that exist in brains? Why couldn't there be organisms from other planets or other solar systems who had minds but had a different chemistry from ours?

The difficulties of behaviorism and of the identity theory led to a new theory, called "functionalism," which is supposed to combine the best features of physicalism and behaviorism, while avoiding many of their difficulties. Functionalism is the most widely held theory of the relation between mind and body among philosophers today. According to its proponents, such as Hilary Putnam and David Lewis, mental states are physical states all right, but they are defined as "mental" not because of their physical constitution but because of their causal relations. We all know of concepts that can be defined functionally, in terms of their causal relations, and we should understand mental concepts by analogy with such concepts.

Think of clocks and carburetors, for example. All clocks and carburetors are physical objects, but they can be made out of different kinds of materials. Something is a clock or a carburetor in virtue of what it does, of what its causal relations are, and not in virtue of the materials it is composed of. Any material will do, provided it does the job (or "functions") so as to produce a specific result, in these cases to tell the time or to mix air and fuel. The situation is essentially the same, the functionalists argue, with mental states. All beliefs and desires are physical states of physical "systems," but the systems can be made out of different kinds of materials. Something is a belief or a desire in virtue of what it does, what its causal relations are, and not in virtue of the materials that its system is composed of. So brains, computers, extraterrestrials, and no doubt other "systems" can have minds provided they have states with the right causal relations.

Here is how a typical functionalist analysis goes. Suppose I believe that it is raining. That belief will be a state of my brain, but a computer or some other system might have the same belief although it has a completely different physical/ chemical composition. So what fact about my brain state makes it that belief? The functionalist answer is that a state of a system—human, computer, or otherwise—is a belief that it is raining if the state has the right causal relations. For example, my belief is a state of my brain caused by my looking out the window when rain is falling from the sky, and this state together with my desire not to get wet (another functional state of my brain) causes a certain sort of output behavior, such as my carrying an umbrella. A belief, then, is any physical state of any physical system which has certain sorts of physical causes, and together with certain sorts of other functional states such as desires, has certain sorts of physical effects.

And remember, none of these causes and effects is to be thought of as having any mental component. They are just physical sequences. The functionalist is emphatically not saying that a belief is an irreducible mental state which *in addition* has these causal relations, but rather that being a belief *consists* entirely in having these causal relations. A belief can consist of a bunch of neuron firings, voltage levels in a computer, green slime in a Martian, *or anything else*, provided that it is part of the right sort of pattern of cause-and-effect relations. A belief, as such, is just a something, an X, that is part of a pattern of causal relations, and it is defined as a belief because of its position in the pattern of causal relations. This pattern is called the "functional organization" of a system, and for a system to have a belief is just for it to have the right functional organization. A functional organization of a system takes a physical input, processes it through a sequence of internal cause-and-effect relations within the system, and produces a physical output.

The word "functionalism" may be confusing because it means many different things in many different disciplines; but in the philosophy of mind, as we have seen, it has a fairly precise meaning. Functionalism, for contemporary philosophers, is the view that mental states are functional states and functional states are physical states; but they are physical states defined as functional states in virtue of their causal relations.

Nobody ever became a functionalist by reflecting on his or her most deeply felt beliefs and desires, much less their hopes, fears, loves, hates, pains, and anxieties. The theory is, in my view, utterly implausible, but to understand its appeal you have to see it in historical context. Dualism seems unscientific and therefore unacceptable; behaviorism and physicalism in their traditional versions have failed. To its adherents, functionalism seems to combine the best features of each. If you are a materialist, functionalism may seem the only available alternative, and this helps explain why it is the the most widely held theory in the philosophy of mind today. In its version linked to the use of computers, it has also become the dominant theory in the new discipline of cognitive science.

The central argument of the cognitive theorists who espouse functionalism is that a functional state in the brain is exactly like a computational state of a computer. What matters in both cases is not the physical features of the state, whether it is a pattern of neuron firings or voltage levels, but the pattern of causal relations. Furthermore, it seems we have a perfect model of functional organization in the computer program: a program can be described as being a functional organization of the hardware—i.e., the program provides the organization of the hardware which causes it to produce a desired result. Nowadays most functionalists would say that mental states are "information-processing" states of a computer. According to the extreme version of computer functionalism, which I have baptized "Strong Artificial Intelligence," or "Strong AI," the brain is a computer and the mind is a computer program implemented in the brain. Mental states are just program states of the brain. Therefore, according to what is now a widely shared view, mental states are to be analyzed in a way which is, at the same time, materialist, functionalist, dependent on information processing, and computationalist.

But anybody who holds such a view has a special problem with consciousness. As with the behaviorist analysis of pain, it seems wildly implausible to think that my conscious feeling of pain consists entirely in functionally analyzed program states of a digital computer in my skull. When it comes to conscious feelings such as pain, the difference between functionalists and the rest of us comes out most sharply. According to our ordinary scientific, common-sense conception:

1. Pains are unpleasant sensations. That is, they are unpleasant, inner, qualitative, subjective experiences.

2. They are caused by specific neurobiological processes in the brain and the rest of the nervous system.

The functionalist has to deny both of these claims. He has to say:

1. Pains are physical states that are parts of patterns of functional organization in brains or anything else. In

human beings the functional organization is this: certain input stimuli, such as injuries, cause physical states of the nervous system (according to computer functionalism these are computational, information-processing states) and these in turn cause certain sorts of physical output behavior.

2. In humans, as in any other system, these functionally organized physical states don't cause pains, they just are pains.

Philosophers sympathetic to the functionalist project have a choice when they come to the problem of explaining consciousness: either give up on functionalism and accept the irreducibility of consciousness, or stay with functionalism and deny the irreducibility of consciousness. Thomas Nagel is an example of a philosopher who rejects functionalism because of the problem of consciousness. Dennett rejects consciousness in favor of functionalism.[2]

2.

We can now see one of the reasons why *The Conscious Mind* by the philosopher David J. Chalmers has been getting much attention, and has been a subject of debate at conferences of philosophers and cognitive scientists.[3] The peculiarity of his position is that he wants to accept both approaches at once. That is, he accepts the entire materialist, functionalist story— Strong AI and all—as an account of the mind up to the point

---

2. See Thomas Nagel, "What is it like to be a bat?" in *Mortal Questions* (Cambridge University Press, 1979), pp. 165–180; see the discussion of Dennett in chapter 5.
3. *The Conscious Mind: In Search of a Fundamental Theory* (Oxford University Press, 1996).

where he reaches consciousness; but then to his general commitment to functionalism he wants to tack on consciousness, which he says is not subject to functionalist analysis. In his view, the material world, with a functional analysis of mental concepts, has an irreducible nonfunctionalist consciousness mysteriously tacked on to it. I call this "peculiar" because functionalism evolved precisely to avoid admitting the irreducible existence of consciousness and of other mental phenomena, and hence to avoid dualism. Chalmers wants both: functionalism and dualism. He summarizes his position as follows: "One can believe that consciousness arises from functional organization but is not a functional state. The view that I advocate has this form—we might call it *nonreductive functionalism.* It might be seen as a way of combining functionalism and property dualism" (p. 249). And even more succinctly, "Cognition can be explained functionally; consciousness resists such explanation" (p. 172).

The situation is made more peculiar by the fact that (1) he uses standard arguments advanced by various authors against functionalism to prove that functionalism can't account for consciousness, and (2) he then refuses to accept similar arguments as general arguments against functionalism. For example, one argument advanced by various philosophers, including Ned Block and myself, is that the functionalist would be forced to say that all kinds of inappropriate systems have mental states. According to the functionalist view, a system made of beer cans, or ping-pong balls, or the population of China as a whole, could have mental states such as beliefs, desires, pains, and itches. But that seems counterintuitive.

Chalmers says the functional organization by itself is not yet consciousness. Consciousness has to be added to the functional organization. But the organization provides the elements of mental states in their non-conscious forms; and later on he tries to show how it "gives rise" to consciousness, as we will see. Although he believes that functional organization isn't the same thing as consciousness, he thinks the two always go together. Here is what he writes:

> Whether the organization is realized in silicon chips, in the population of China, or in beer cans and ping-pong balls does not matter. As long as the functional organization is right, conscious experience will be determined. [p. 249]

Why does he say this? That is, what has led to this odd marriage of computer functionalism and property dualism? I think *The Conscious Mind* is a symptom of a certain desperation in cognitive studies today. On the one hand it is hard to give up on computer functionalism because it is the main research program in cognitive science; but on the other hand, no one has been able to give even a remotely plausible functionalist account of consciousness. Chalmers simply tacks consciousness onto his general commitment to functionalism. His book, as I will argue, does not give an acceptable account of consciousness, but it has been widely heralded as some kind of a breakthrough. I believe this is because it seems to combine functionalism, which people want on ideological grounds, with an acknowledgment of the existence and irreducibility of consciousness, which many people in cognitive studies are—at last—prepared to admit.

Chalmers begins his book by insisting that we should take consciousness seriously and by arguing for its irreducibility. So far, so good.

His arguments for the irreducibility of consciousness are developments and extensions of arguments used by Thomas Nagel, Frank Jackson, Saul Kripke, myself, and others. Perhaps the simplest argument, and the one on which I believe he depends most, rests on the logical possibility of unconscious zombies. If it is logically possible, in the sense of being not self-contradictory, to imagine that there could be zombies that were organized just as we are and had exactly our behavior patterns, but were totally devoid of consciousness, then it follows that our consciousness cannot logically consist simply in our behavior or functional organization. In describing such a case earlier I have asked the reader to imagine that his or her brain is replaced by silicon chips that reproduce behavior but without the consciousness that typically goes with the behavior.[4] The silicon chips, for example, might transmit stimuli that make us get up and cross the room, but we might not be conscious we are doing so. If such a thing is imaginable, and it surely is, then consciousness cannot be just a matter of behavior or functional organization. Suppose for example that when my brain is replaced by silicon chips the resultant machine utters such sounds as "I fell in love with you at first sight" or "I find this line of poetry thrilling," even though the "system" has no conscious feeling whatever. The machine makes the sounds, but has no more feeling than a tape recorder or a voice synthesizer that makes such sounds. Such a system is logically

---

4. John R. Searle, *The Rediscovery of the Mind* (MIT Press, 1992), p. 65 ff.

possible, in the sense that there is nothing self-contradictory about the supposition.

Chalmers takes the argument one step further, in a direction I would not be willing to go. He asks us to imagine a case where the whole system is physically identical to a normal human being down to the last molecule but is without any conscious states at all. On my view such a case would be impossible because we know that the structure and function of the brain are causally sufficient to produce consciousness. Chalmers would agree that such a case is biologically impossible, but, he points out, there is nothing logically necessary about the laws of biology. We can imagine a world in which the laws are different. It is certainly logically possible, in the sense of being not self-contradictory, to suppose that there could be a world where all the physical particles were exactly like ours, with a zombie doppelgänger for each of us, in which there was no consciousness at all. In such a world, the doppelgänger makes the sounds "I find this line of poetry thrilling" but has no conscious experiences at all. But if so, it seems to Chalmers that consciousness is something additional to and not part of the physical world. If the physical world could be the same without consciousness, then consciousness is not a part of the physical world.

As it stands, this argument is invalid. If I imagine a miraculous world in which the laws of nature are different, I can easily imagine a world which has the same microstructure as ours but has all sorts of different higher-level properties. I can imagine a world in which pigs can fly, and rocks are alive, for example. But the fact that I can imagine these science-fiction cases does not show that life and acts of flying are not physical properties and events. So, in extending the zombie argument Chalmers produces an invalid version. The original version was designed to show that behavior and functional organization by themselves are not sufficient for consciousness. Chalmers uses it to show that in a different world, where the laws of nature are different, you could have all your physical features intact but no consciousness. From this he concludes that consciousness is not a physical property. That conclusion does not follow.

3.

Before examining Chalmers's explanation for the existence of consciousness, let us remind ourselves of how consciousness works in real life. In a typical case, here is how I get a conscious state of pain: I hit my thumb with a hammer. This causes me to feel a conscious, unpleasant sensation of pain. My pain in turn causes me to yell "Ouch!" The pain itself is caused by a sequence of specific neurobiological events in the nervous system beginning at the sensory receptors and ending in the brain, probably in the thalamus, other basal regions of the brain, and the somato-sensory cortex. There is of course much more to be said and much more to know about the neurobiological details, but the story I just told is true as far as it goes, and we know that something like it must be true before we ever start philosophizing about these questions. But Chalmers can't accept any of it. Because of his metaphysical distinction between consciousness and physical reality, he does not think that the specific neurobiological features of brains have any special causal role in the production of conscious pains, and on his account conscious pains certainly can't provide the causal explanation of physical behavior. (Later on it will turn out that for Chalmers everything in the universe "gives rise" to consciousness, so brains do too, but this has nothing to do with the specific neurobiology of brains. It is all a matter of functional organization.)

Given his property dualism and his functionalism, what is he going to say? His property dualism would seem to require him to say that pain is not part of the physical world at all. For the property dualist, pain is a mental, not a physical, phenomenon. His functionalism would seem to require that he say that pain consists entirely in a physical state causally related to other physical states. But he has to say *something* in order to account for the very existence of consciousness as a phenomenon distinct from functional organization, once he has accepted both the functionalist analysis of the mind and the irreducibility of consciousness.

In the end he says there are really two meanings to "pain": one a physical, functionalist meaning, according to which pain is not a conscious state at all, and the other, a meaning dependent on consciousness, i.e., a meaning in which pains are unpleasant sensations. His problem then is to explain the relation between the two, and he thinks his only hope is to exploit the "principle of structural coherence." This principle states that the structure of consciousness is mirrored by the structure of functional organization and functional organization is mirrored by the structure of consciousness. Using this perfect correlation, he wants to explain conscious states in terms of functional states. The result is the combination of functionalism and property dualism I mentioned earlier.

He can't quite bring himself to say that functional states *cause* conscious states, because dualists always have a hard time with a causal relation between the two realms. So he says, unhelpfully, that "consciousness arises in virtue of the *functional organization* of the brain" (p. 248).

This is his account of consciousness. It is important to keep reminding ourselves of how counterintuitive, how bizarre, it really is. In real life there is indeed a pretty good match between "functional organization" and consciousness, at least where humans are concerned, but that is because typically parts of the organization cause consciousness and consciousness in turn causes other parts of the organization. Remember, "functional organization" just refers to the pattern of physical causes and effects that begins with input stimuli and ends with output behavior. *You need consciousness to explain the coherence and not the coherence to explain the consciousness.* Think of the match between functional organization and consciousness in the sequence: Hammer-Thumb-Pain-Ouch. The hammer hitting the thumb causes a sequence of neuron firings which eventually cause the conscious experience of pain, and the pain in turn causes one to say "Ouch!" The functional organization as such is quite insufficient to account for the causation of pain. Pains are caused crucially by what happens inside the nervous systems of humans and other animals. And in inanimate objects, cars and thermostats for example, you can have as much functional organization as you like, but there is still no consciousness and no pain.

As far as I can see, Chalmers advances only one substantial argument for the claim that there must be a perfect match between consciousness and functional organization.

The argument comes in two versions: the argument from "fading qualia" and from "dancing qualia" ("qualia" refers to the qualitative aspect of conscious states), but they are essentially the same. The basic idea of the argument is to show that there could not be a mismatch between functional organization and consciousness, because if there were it would be possible to imagine a system's conscious states fading out ("fading qualia") even though its functional organization and hence its behavior remained constant. And it would also be possible to imagine a system's conscious states changing in a way that was not systematically related to its behavior ("dancing qualia"). But these, he says, are impossible because any change in mental content must be "mirrored in a change in functional organization" and therefore in behavior.

But this argument just begs the question by repeating the point at issue and does not establish it. Suppose that a pattern of functional organization could be constructed so that a system which was unconscious behaved as if it were conscious. Just imagine, for example, a robot constructed so that it behaved as if it were conscious, even though it isn't. Suppose furthermore, as I think is indeed the case, that consciousness is caused by brain processes and that this robot has nothing like a brain structure sufficient to cause consciousness. Then you have a mismatch between functional organization and consciousness. The robot has the functional organization but no consciousness. Nothing in Chalmers's argument shows such a thing to be impossible, and therefore nothing in his argument shows that functional organization and consciousness must always go together.

Furthermore, we know independently that you can get

all sorts of breaks between specific forms of behavior and specific forms of consciousness. For example, some patients with Guillain-Barre syndrome have a normal conscious inner life which they are unable to express in behavior at all. They are totally paralyzed to the point that the doctors think the patients are unconscious, indeed totally brain-dead. The "functional organization" is inappropriate, because the terrified and paralyzed patient is fully conscious, but can't manifest the consciousness in behavior.

Even if there were a perfect match, moreover, that would still not be an explanation of consciousness. We would still need to know: How does it work? How does the *organization*, which is specified purely formally and without any reference to specific materials, cause the feeling? And in any case the whole idea runs counter to everything we know from brain science. We know independently that brain processes *cause* consciousness.

4.

I believe there is not much to be said in favor of either functionalism or property dualism, but Chalmers's book shows the extra absurd consequences of trying to combine the two. To his credit he follows out the logical consequences of his views, even when doing so leads him to conclusions that are quite breathtakingly implausible. Here are some of them, in ascending order of implausibility:

1. It turns out that, in general, *psychological terms*—"pain," "belief," "hope," "fear," "desire," etc.—*have two quite distinct meanings, a materialist, functionalist meaning referring*

to material entities and a consciousness meaning referring to conscious entities. According to the materialist meaning, having a pain, for example, is analyzed functionally, in the way I described earlier. There is nothing conscious about pains on this definition. There are just physical patterns of functional organization, whereby certain sorts of input stimuli cause certain sorts of output behavior. But "pain" also has another completely independent meaning where it refers to our inner feelings—the conscious sensation that actually feels painful. On the materialist meaning, according to Chalmers, an unconscious zombie has pains, fears, and desires as well as anxiety, depression, love, and terror. He, she, or it has these in exactly the same materialist sense as the conscious doppelgänger, even though the zombie feels absolutely nothing. He, she, or it just lacks these feelings in their consciousness sense.[5]

Chalmers tells us not to worry about the fact that the two sorts of phenomena are independent, because in the real world they almost always go together, according to the principle of coherence that I mentioned earlier. But it turns out that the coherence is not much help to us because:

2. *It now appears that consciousness is explanatorily irrelevant to everything physical that happens in the world. In*

---

5. Chalmers describes the materialist phenomena as matters of "awareness" or of a "psychological" sense of the words. But on the ordinary meaning of these words, that can't be a correct use of them, because without any consciousness at all there is no possibility of awareness or psychological reality. I have therefore described his distinction as that between a materialist sense of the words and a sense based on consciousness, and correspondingly a materialist and a conscious reality corresponding to the words. In spite of its inelegance, I think this is a more accurate and less misleading way of characterizing the distinction he thinks he has found.

particular, consciousness is irrelevant to the explanation of human behavior. Given his dualistic conviction that consciousness is not part of the physical world, and his claim that the "physical domain is causally closed" (p. 161), it is not easy to see how he could avoid this conclusion. In any case here is what he says: "However the metaphysics of causation turns out, it seems relatively straightforward that a physical explanation of behavior can be given that neither appeals to nor implies the existence of consciousness" (p. 177). And again, "The very fact that [conscious] experience can be coherently subtracted from any causal account implies that [conscious] experience is superfluous in the *explanation* of behavior...." (pp. 158–159). The physical universe is causally self-sufficient. Physical events can have only physical explanations, and consciousness is not physical, so consciousness plays no explanatory role whatsoever. If, for example, you think you ate because you were consciously hungry, or got married because you were consciously in love with your prospective spouse, or withdrew your hand from the fire because you consciously felt a pain, or spoke up at the meeting because you consciously disagreed with the main speaker, you are mistaken in every case. In each case the effect was a physical event and therefore must have an entirely physical explanation. Though consciousness exists, it plays no role either in the explanation of your behavior or of anything else.

It gets worse:

3. *Even your own judgments about your consciousness cannot be explained—neither entirely nor even in part—by your consciousness.* So, for example, if you say, "I am now in pain," or even "I am now conscious," the fact of your being in pain

or conscious is explanatorily irrelevant—totally irrelevant —to what you say. The reason is that your utterance is a physical event in the world like any other and has to be explained entirely by physical causes. Your zombie doppelgänger, who is totally devoid of consciousness, is uttering the same sentences that you are and for the same reasons. Indeed we can say that Chalmers wrote a book defending the irreducibility of his conscious states, but that, on his view, his conscious states and their irreducibility could have no explanatory relevance at all to his writing the book. They are explanatorily irrelevant because his writing the book is a physical event like any other and thus must have a purely physical explanation.

Even worse is yet to come:

What is it about the functional state that does the job of "giving rise" to consciousness? It is, he says, information; not information in the ordinary common-sense meaning of the word in which I have information about how to get to San Jose, but in an extended "information theory" sense, in which any physical "*difference that makes a difference*" in the world is information (p. 281). According to Chalmers's conception of information, rain hitting the ground contains "information," because it makes changes in the ground. But if consciousness arises from information in this extended sense, then:

4. *Consciousness is everywhere.* The thermostat is conscious, the stomach is conscious, there are lots of conscious systems in my brain of which I am totally unconscious, the Milky Way is conscious, there are various conscious systems in any stone... and so on. The reason is that all of these systems contain "information" in his extended sense.

This absurd view, called panpsychism, is a direct consequence of attempting to explain consciousness in terms of "information" in this denuded technical sense of the word. In a section of his book about the conscious life of thermostats, and cheerfully called "What is it like to be a thermostat?" Chalmers tells us that "certainly it will not be very interesting to be a thermostat" (p. 293). And: "Perhaps we can think of these states by analogy to our experiences of black, white, and gray" (p. 294). But he faces up to the obvious consequences: if thermostats are conscious, then everything is.

> If there is experience associated with thermostats, there is probably experience *everywhere*: wherever there is causal interaction, there is information, and wherever there is information, there is experience. One can find information states in a rock—when it expands and contracts, for example—or even in the different states of an electron. So if the unrestricted double-aspect principle is correct, there will be [conscious] experience associated with a rock or an electron. [p. 297]

It is to Chalmers's credit that he sees the consequences of his views; it is not to his credit that he fails to see that they are absurd. In general when faced with a *reductio ad absurdum* argument he just accepts the absurdity. It is as if someone got the result that 2 + 2 = 7 and said, "Well, maybe 2 plus 2 does equal 7." For example, consider his account of Ned Block's Chinese Nation argument, which I mentioned earlier. Block argues against functionalism as follows: if functionalism were true and functional organization were sufficient for having a mind, we could imagine the population of China as a whole carrying out the steps in some functional program for mental states. One citizen per neuron, for example. But the population as a whole would not thereby constitute a mind, nor would the population as a whole be conscious. Chalmers's response is to bite the bullet and say, yes, the population as a whole constitutes a mind and is conscious as a unit. It is one thing to bite the odd bullet here and there, but this book consumes an entire arsenal.

I have so far been considering only those absurdities that he explicitly commits himself to. These are bad enough, but when at one point he warns the reader that he is about to enter "the realm of speculative metaphysics" (p. 302) (unlike the previous 300 pages?), he goes off the rails completely. Maybe, he tells us, the whole universe is a giant computer. Perhaps the entire world is made up of "pure information" (p. 303) and perhaps the information is ultimately "phenomenal or protophenomenal" (p. 305). What this means is that maybe the world is entirely made up of tiny little bits of consciousness. Such views, he assures us, are "strangely beautiful" (p. 303). I, for one, did not find them so; I found them strangely self-indulgent.

5.

When confronted with these absurdities, Chalmers has two standard rhetorical responses. First he claims that it is equally implausible to suppose that brains, lumps of gray matter in our skulls, can be conscious. "Whoever would have thought that this hunk of gray matter would be the sort of thing that

could produce vivid subjective experiences?" (p. 251). But if
they can, as they do, then why not thermostats and all the rest?
Secondly he tries to shift the burden of argument. *We* are supposed to tell *him* why thermostats are *not* conscious:

> Someone who finds it "crazy" to suppose that a thermo-
> stat might have [conscious] experiences at least owes us
> an account of just *why* it is crazy. Presumably this is
> because there is a property that thermostats lack that is
> obviously required for experience; but for my part no
> such property reveals itself as obvious. Perhaps there is a
> crucial ingredient in processing that the thermostat lacks
> that a mouse possesses, or that a mouse lacks and a
> human possesses, but I can see no such ingredient that
> is *obviously* required for experience, and indeed it is not
> obvious that such an ingredient must exist. [p. 295]

The answers to each of these questions can be briefly
stated; the deeper question is why they didn't occur to
Chalmers. First, where the brute facts of biology are concerned, arguments about plausibility are irrelevant. It is just a
plain fact about nature that brains cause consciousness. It does
not seem at all implausible to me because I know, independently of any philosophical argument, that it happens. If it
still seems implausible to the biologically uninformed, so
much the worse for them. But second, we know that brains
cause consciousness by means of their quite specific, though
still imperfectly understood, neurobiological structures and
functions. Now it follows from the fact that brains cause consciousness that anything else capable of causing consciousness

would have to have the relevant *causal* powers at least equal to the minimal powers that human and animal brains have for the production of consciousness. We do not know the details of how brains do it, but we know that they have some powers to get us over the threshold of consciousness. That much causal power must be possessed by any successful artifact.

This point is a trivial logical consequence of what we know about nature. It is just like saying: if you want to build a diesel engine that will drive my car as fast as my gas engine, your engine will have to have at least an equivalent power output. You might build an artificial brain using some other medium—silicon chips or vacuum tubes, for example—but whatever the medium, it must at least equal the brain's threshold capacity to cause consciousness. Now in light of this, how are we supposed to think of thermostats? It is not self-contradictory or logically absurd to suppose a thermostat could be conscious; but for anyone who takes biology seriously it is quite out of the question. What features are we supposed to look for when we take our thermostat apart to see how it might cause subjective states of consciousness? The thermostat on my wall does not have enough structure even to be a remote candidate for consciousness.

But worse yet, for thermostats as a class there is nothing to look for, because "thermostat" does not name a type of physical object. Any mechanism that responds to changes in temperature and can activate some other mechanism at particular temperatures can be used as a thermostat, and all sorts of things can do that. My thermostat is a bimetallic strip, but you can buy thermostats that use mercury expansion to complete a circuit, or for that matter you can get someone to watch the thermometer and turn the furnace on and off when the thermometer reaches certain temperatures. All of these systems could equally be called "thermostats," but what they do is not even a remote candidate for achieving the causal powers of the brain, and with the exception of the system containing a human brain, they have nothing individually for which it would be other than neurobiologically preposterous to suggest that it does what the brain does by way of causing consciousness.

6.

What has gone wrong? Chalmers thinks his surprising results are a logical consequence of taking consciousness and its irreducibility seriously. I think that these results follow not from taking consciousness seriously as such, but from conjoining a peculiar form of the irreducibility thesis, property dualism, with the contemporary functionalist, computationalist account of the mind, an account that identifies mental function with information processing. Suppose we jettison functionalism in all its forms and with it the traditional metaphysical categories of dualism, monism, etc., that historically led to functionalism. If we get rid of both of these mistakes, we can continue to take consciousness seriously but without Chalmers's absurd results. Specifically:

1. There are not two definitions of the psychological terms such as "belief," "desire," "pain," and "love," one definition referring to conscious states, one to material states. Rather, only systems capable of consciousness can have any psychology at all, and though all of us have plenty of unconscious mental states, unconscious beliefs and desires for example, we under-

stand these as mental states, because we understand them as potentially conscious, as the sorts of things that might have been conscious but are not because of repression, brain damage, or perhaps just because we fell asleep.

2. We are not compelled to say that consciousness is "explanatorily irrelevant," i.e., that consciousness plays no role in explaining behavior. Nature might conceivably turn out to be that way, but it is most unlikely. On the available evidence, consciousness is crucial to explaining behavior in the way that is typical of other higher-level features of physical systems, such as the solidity of the pistons in my car engine, for example. Both consciousness and solidity depend on lower-level microelements, but both are causally efficacious. You can't run a car engine with a piston made of butter, and you can't write a book if you are unconscious.

3. Once we accept that consciousness is essential to the explanation of human behavior, then a fortiori it is essential where its own representation is concerned. My judgment that I am in pain is explained by my being in pain, my judgment that I am conscious is explained by my being conscious, and the explanation of Chalmers's writing a book about consciousness is that he had certain conscious convictions about consciousness that he consciously wanted to convey.

4. There is not the slightest reason to adopt panpsychism, the view that everything in the universe is conscious. Consciousness is above all a biological phenomenon and is as restricted in its biology as the secretion of bile or the digestion of carbohydrates. Of all the absurd results in Chalmers's book, panpsychism is the most absurd and provides us with a clue that something is radically wrong with the thesis that implies it.

7.

Some books are important not because they solve a problem or even address it in a way that points to a solution, but because they are symptomatic of the confusions of the time. Chalmers's book has been hailed as a great step forward in the philosophy of mind: it was much discussed among the hundreds of academics that attended a recent conference on consciousness in Tucson; it has been quoted in the pages of *Time* magazine; and the jacket of the book contains encomia from various famous philosophers. Yet if I understand it correctly, the book is a mass of confusions. What is going on? These confusions can only be understood in light of our peculiar intellectual history. Where the mind is concerned, we have inherited an obsolete Cartesian vocabulary and with it a set of categories that include "dualism," "monism," "materialism," and all the rest of it. If you take these categories seriously, if you think our questions have to be asked and answered in these terms, and if you also accept modern science (is there a choice?), I believe you will eventually be forced to some version of materialism. But materialism in its traditional forms is more or less obviously false, above all in its failure to account for consciousness. So eventually you are likely to be backed into the corner of functionalism or computationalism: the brain is a computer and the mind is a computer program. I think this view is also false, and it is obviously false about consciousness. What to do? Until recently most people concerned with these questions tried either not to think about consciousness or to deny its existence. Nowadays that is not so easy. Chalmers offers this much: he thinks you can keep your functionalism but you should add property dualism to it. The result, in my view, is to trade one false doctrine for two. I believe Chalmers has provided a *reductio ad absurdum* of the combination.

The correct approach, which we are still only groping toward in the cognitive sciences, is to forget about the obsolete Cartesian categories and keep reminding ourselves that the brain is a biological organ, like any other, and consciousness is as much a biological process as digestion or photosynthesis.

APPENDIX

An Exchange with David Chalmers

Following the publication of this chapter in The New York Review of Books, *David Chalmers and I had the following exchange.*

DAVID CHALMERS writes:

In my book *The Conscious Mind*, I deny a number of claims that John Searle finds "obvious," and I make some claims that he finds "absurd." But if the mind–body problem has taught us anything, it is that nothing about consciousness is obvious, and that one person's obvious truth is another person's absurdity. So instead of throwing around this sort of language, it is best to examine the claims themselves and the arguments that I give for them, to see whether Searle says anything of substance that touches them.

The first is my claim that consciousness is a nonphysical feature of the world. I resisted this claim for a long time, before concluding that it is forced on one by a sound argument. The argument is complex, but the basic idea is simple: the physical structure of the world—the exact distribution of particles, fields, and forces in spacetime—is logically consistent with the absence of consciousness, so the presence of consciousness is a further fact about our world. Searle says this argument is "invalid": he suggests that the physical structure of the world is equally consistent with the addition of flying pigs, but that it does not follow that flying is nonphysical.

Here Searle makes two elementary mistakes. First, he gets the form of the argument wrong. To show that flying is nonphysical, we would need to show that the world's physical structure is consistent with the *absence* of flying. From the fact that one can *add* flying pigs to the world, nothing follows. Second, the scenario he describes is not consistent. A world with flying pigs would have a lot of extra matter hovering meters above the earth, for example, so it could not possibly have the same physical structure as ours. Putting these points together: the idea of a world physically identical to ours but without flying, or without pigs, or without rocks, is self-contradictory. But there is no contradiction in the idea of a world physically identical to ours without consciousness, as Searle himself admits.

The underlying point is that the position of pigs—and almost everything else about the world—is logically derivable from the world's physical structure, but the presence of consciousness is not. So to explain why and how brains support consciousness, an account of the brain alone is not enough; to bridge the gap, one needs to add independent "bridging" laws. One can resist this conclusion only by adopting a hard-line deflationism about consciousness. That path has its own problems, but in any case it is not open to Searle, who holds that consciousness is irreducible. Irreducibility has its consequences. Consistency requires that one face them directly.

The next issue is my nonreductive functionalism. This bridging law claims that systems with the same functional organization have the same sort of conscious experiences. My detailed argument for this claim is not recognizable in the trivial argument that Searle presents as mine and rebuts. The basic idea, presented in chapter 7 of the book but ignored by Searle, is that if the claim is false, then there can be massive changes in conscious experience which a subject can never notice. (Searle's own position is rebutted on p. 258.) He also points to patients with Guillain-Barre syndrome as a counterexample to my claim, but this once again gets the logic wrong. My claim concerns functionally identical beings, so it is irrelevant to point to people who function differently. I certainly do not claim that beings whose functioning differs from ours are unconscious.

The final issue is panpsychism: the claim that some degree of consciousness is associated with every system in the natural world. Here Searle misstates my view: he says that I am "explicitly committed" to this position, when I merely explore it and remain agnostic; and he says incorrectly that it is an implication of property dualism and nonreductive functionalism. One can quite consistently embrace those views and reject panpsychism, so the latter could not possibly function as a "*reductio ad absurdum*" of the former. I note also that the view which I describe as "strangely beautiful," and which Searle describes as "strangely self-indulgent," is a view I reject.

I do argue that panpsychism is not as unreasonable as is often supposed, and that there is no knockdown argument against it. Searle helps confirm the latter claim: while protesting "absurdity," his arguments against panpsychism have no substance. He declares that to be conscious, a system must have the right "causal powers," which turn out to be the powers to produce consciousness: true, but trivial and entirely unhelpful. And he says that simple systems (such as thermostats) do not have the "structure" required for consciousness; but this is precisely the claim at issue, and he provides no argument to support it (if we knew what sort of structure were required for consciousness, the mind–body problem would be half-solved). So we are left where we started. Panpsychism remains counterintuitive, but it cannot be ruled out at the start of inquiry.

In place of substantive arguments, Searle provides gut reactions: every time he disagrees with a view I discuss, he calls it "absurd." In the case of panpsychism (a view not endorsed by me), many might agree. In other cases, the word is devalued: it is not even surprising, for example, that mental terms such as "perception" are ambiguous between a process and a subjective experience; and given that a trillion interacting neurons can result in consciousness, there is no special absurdity in the idea that a trillion interacting silicon chips or humans might do the same. I do bite one bullet, in accepting that brain-based explanations of behavior can be given that do not invoke or imply consciousness (although this is not to say that consciousness is causally irrelevant). But Searle's own view on irreducibility would commit him to this view too, if he could only draw the implication.

Once we factor out mistakes, misrepresentations, and gut feelings, we are left with not much more than Searle's all-purpose critique: "the brain causes consciousness." Although this mantra (repeated at least ten times) is apparently intended as a source of great wisdom, it settles almost nothing that is at issue. It is entirely compatible with all of my views: we just need to distinguish cause from effect, and to note that it does not imply that *only* the brain causes consciousness. Indeed, Searle's claim is simply a statement of the problem, not a solution. If one accepts it, the real questions are: Why does the brain cause consciousness? In virtue of which of its properties? What are the relevant causal laws? Searle has nothing to say about these questions. A real answer requires a theory: not just a theory of the brain, but also a detailed theory of the laws that bridge brain and consciousness. Without fulfilling this project, on which I make a start in my book, our understanding of consciousness will always remain at a primitive level.

(Further remarks and a further reply to Searle are at http://ling.ucsc.edu/~chalmers/nyrb/)

JOHN SEARLE replies:

I am grateful that David Chalmers has replied to my review of his book, and I will try to answer every substantive point he makes. In my review, I pointed out that his combination of property dualism and functionalism led him to some "implausible" consequences. I did not claim, as he thinks, that these consequences are logically implied by his joint acceptance of property dualism and functionalism; rather, I said that when he worked out the details of his position, these views emerged. Property dualism is the view that there are two metaphysically distinct kinds of properties in the world, mental and physical. Functionalism is the view that the mental states of a "system," whether human, machine, or otherwise, consist in physical functional states of that system; and functional states are defined in terms of sets of causal relations.

Here are four of his claims that I found unacceptable:

1. Chalmers thinks each of the psychological words, "pain," "belief," etc., has two completely independent meanings: one where it refers to nonconscious functional processes, and one where it refers to states of consciousness.

2. Consciousness is explanatorily irrelevant to anything physical that happens in the world. If you think you are reading this because you consciously want to read it, Chalmers says you are mistaken. Physical events can have only physical explanations, so consciousness plays no explanatory role whatever in your behavior or anyone else's.

3. Even your own claims about your own consciousness are not explained by consciousness. If you say "I am in pain," when you are in pain, it cannot be because you are in pain that you said it.

4. Consciousness is everywhere. Everything in the universe is conscious.

This view is called "panpsychism," and is the view that I characterized as "absurd."

Now, what has Chalmers to say about these points in his reply? He says that my opposition to these views is just a "gut reaction" without argument. Well, I tried to make my arguments clear, and in any case for views as implausible as these I believe the onus of proof is on him. But just to make my position as clear as possible let me state my arguments precisely:

1. As a native speaker of English, I know what these words mean, and there is no meaning of the word "pain," for example, where for every conscious pain in the world there must be a correlated nonconscious functional state which is also called "pain." On the standard dictionary definition, "pain" means unpleasant sensation, and that definition agrees with my usage as well as that of my fellow English speakers. He thinks otherwise. The onus is surely on him to prove his claim.

2. If we know anything about how human psychology works, we know that conscious desires, inclinations, preferences, etc., affect human behavior. I frequently drink, for example, because I am thirsty. If you get a philosophical result that is inconsistent with this fact, as he does, you had better go back and examine your premises. Of course, it is conceivable that science might show that we are mistaken about this, but to do so would require a major scientific revolution and such a revolution could not be established by the armchair theorizing in which he engages.

3. In my own case, when I am in pain, I sometimes say "I am in pain," precisely because I am in pain. I experience all three: the pain, my reporting the pain, and my reporting it for the reason that I have it. These are just facts about my own experiences. I take it other people's experiences are not all that different from mine. What sort of arguments does he want in addition to these plain facts? Once again, if you get a result

that denies this, then you had better go back and look at your premises. His conclusions are best understood not as the wonderful discoveries he thinks; rather each is a *reductio ad absurdum* of his premises.

4. What about panpsychism, his view that consciousness is in rocks, thermostats, and electrons (his examples), indeed everywhere? I am not sure what he expects as an argument against this view. The only thing one can say is that we know too much about how the world works to take this view seriously as a scientific hypothesis. Does he want me to tell him what we know? Perhaps he does.

We know that human and some animal brains are conscious. Those *living systems* with *certain sorts of nervous systems* are the only systems in the world that we know for a fact are conscious. We also know that consciousness in these systems is caused by quite specific neurobiological processes. We do not know the details of how the brain does it, but we know, for example, that if you interfere with the processes in certain ways—general anesthetic, or a blow to the head, for example —the patient becomes unconscious and if you get some of the brain processes going again the patient regains consciousness. The processes are causal processes. They cause consciousness. Now, for someone seriously interested in how the world actually works, thermostats, rocks, and electrons are not even candidates to have anything remotely like these processes, or to have any processes capable of having equivalent causal powers to the specific features of neurobiology. Of course as a science-fiction fantasy we can imagine conscious thermostats, but science fiction is not science. And it is not philosophy either.

The most astonishing thing in Chalmers's letter is the claim that he did not "endorse" panpsychism, that he is "agnostic" about it. Well, in his book he presents extensive arguments for it and defenses of it. Here is what he actually says. First, he tells us that "consciousness arises from functional organization" (p. 249). And what is it about functional organization that does the job? It is, he tells us, "information" in his special sense of that word according to which everything in the world has information in it. "We might put this by suggesting as a basic principle that information (in the actual world) has two aspects, a physical and a phenomenal aspect" (p. 286). The closest he gets to agnosticism is this: "I do not have any knockdown arguments to prove that information is the key to the link between physical processes and conscious experience," but he immediately adds, "but there are some indirect ways of giving support to the idea." Whereupon he gives us several arguments for the double-aspect principle (p. 287). He hasn't proven panpsychism, but it is a hypothesis he thinks is well supported. Since information in his sense is everywhere then consciousness is everywhere. Taken together his premises imply panpsychism. If he argues that functional organization gives rise to consciousness, that it does so in virtue of information, that anything that has information would be conscious and that everything has information, then he is arguing for the view that everything is conscious, by any logic that I am aware of.

And if he is not supporting panpsychism, then why does he devote an entire section of a chapter to "What is it like to be a thermostat?" in which he describes the conscious life of thermostats?

At least part of the section is worth quoting in full:

> Certainly it will not be very interesting to be a thermo-
> stat. The information processing is so simple that we
> should expect the corresponding phenomenal states to
> be equally simple. There will be three primitively differ-
> ent phenomenal states, with no further structure. Perhaps
> we can think of these states by analogy to our experiences
> of black, white, and gray: a thermostat can have an all-
> black phenomenal field, an all-white field, or an all-gray
> field. But even this is to impute far too much structure to
> the thermostat's experiences, by suggesting the dimen-
> sionality of a visual field and the relatively rich natures
> of black, white, and gray. We should really expect some-
> thing much simpler, for which there is no analog in our
> experience. We will likely be unable to sympathetically
> imagine these experiences any better than a blind person
> can imagine sight, or than a human can imagine what it
> is like to be a bat; but we can at least intellectually know
> something about their basic structure. [pp. 293–294]

He then goes on to try to make the conscious life of thermostats more plausible by comparing our inability to appreciate thermostats with our difficulty in understanding the
consciousness of animals. And two pages later he adds, "But
thermostats are really no different from brains here."

What are we to make of his analogy between the consciousness of animals and the consciousness of thermostats?
I do not believe that anyone who writes such prose can be
serious about the results of neurobiology. In any case they do

not exhibit an attitude that is "agnostic" about whether thermostats are conscious. And, according to him, if thermostats are conscious then everything is.

Chalmers genuinely was agnostic about the view that the whole universe consists of little bits of consciousness. He put this forward as a "strangely beautiful" possibility to be taken seriously. Now he tells us it is a view he "rejects." He did not reject it in his book.

The general strategy of Chalmers's book is to present his several basic premises, most importantly, property dualism and functionalism, and then draw the consequences I have described. When he gets such absurd consequences, he thinks they must be true because they follow from the premises. I am suggesting that his conclusions cast doubt on the premises, which are in any case, insufficiently established. So, let's go back and look at his argument for two of his most important premises, "property dualism" and "nonreductive functionalism," the two he mentions in his letter.

In his argument for property dualism, he says, correctly, that you can imagine a world that has the same physical features that our world has—but minus consciousness. Quite so, but in order to imagine such a world, you have to imagine a change in the laws of nature, a change in those laws by which physics and biology cause and realize consciousness. But then, I argued, if you are allowed to mess around with the laws of nature, you can make the same point about flying pigs. If I am allowed to imagine a change in the laws of nature, then I can imagine the laws of nature changed so pigs can fly. He points out, again correctly, that that would involve a change in the distribution of physical features, because now pigs would be up in the air. But my answer to that, which I apparently failed to make clear, is that if consciousness is a physical feature of brains, then the absence of consciousness is *also* a change in the physical features of the world. That is, his argument works to establish property dualism only if it assumes that consciousness is not a physical feature, but that is what the argument was supposed to prove. From the facts of nature, including the laws, you can derive logically that this brain must be conscious. From the facts of nature, including the laws, you can derive that this pig can't fly. The two cases are parallel. The real difference is that consciousness is irreducible. But irreducibility by itself is not a proof of property dualism.

Now I turn to his argument for "nonreductive functionalism." The argument is that systems with the same nonconscious functional organization must have the same sort of conscious experiences. But the argument that he gives for this in his book and repeats in his reply, begs the question. Here is how he summarizes it:

If there were not a perfect match between conscious experiences and functional organization, then there could be massive changes in someone's conscious experiences, which the subject having those experiences would never *notice.* But in this last statement, the word "notice" is not used in the conscious sense of "notice." It refers to the noticing behavior of a nonconscious functional organization. Remember for Chalmers all these words have two meanings, one implying consciousness, one nonconscious functional organization. Thus, the argument begs the question by assuming that radical changes in a person's consciousness, including his conscious noticing, must be matched by changes in the nonconscious functional organization that produces noticing behavior. But that is precisely the point at issue. What the argument has to show, if it is going to work, is that there must be a perfect match between an agent's inner experiences and his external behavior together with the "functional organization" of which the behavior is a part. But he gives no argument for this. The only argument is the question-begging: there must be such a match because otherwise there wouldn't be a match between the external noticing part of the match and the internal experience. He says incorrectly that the Guillain-Barre patients who have consciousness but the wrong functional organization are irrelevant, because they "function differently." But differently from what? As far as their physical behavior is concerned they function exactly like people who are totally unconscious, and thus on his definition they have exactly the same "functional organization" as unconscious people, even though they are perfectly conscious. Remember "functional organization" for him is always nonconscious. The Guillain-Barre patients have the same functional organization, but different consciousness. Therefore there is no perfect match between functional organization and consciousness. Q.E.D.

Chalmers resents the fact that I frequently try to remind him that brains cause consciousness, a claim he calls a "mantra." But I don't think he has fully appreciated its significance. Consciousness is above all a biological phenomenon, like digestion or photosynthesis. This is just a fact of nature that has to be respected by any philosophical account. Of course, in principle we might build a conscious machine out of nonbiological materials. If we can build an artificial heart that pumps blood, why not an artificial brain that causes consciousness?

But the essential step in the project of understanding consciousness and creating it artificially is to figure out in detail how the
brain does it as a specific biological process in real life. Initially,
at least, the answer will have to be given in terms like "synapse," "peptides," "ion channels," "40 hertz," "neuronal maps,"
etc., because those are real features of the real mechanism we
are studying. Later on we might discover more general principles that permit us to abstract away from the biology.

But, and this is the point, Chalmers's candidates for
explaining consciousness, "functional organization" and
"information," are nonstarters, because as he uses them, they
have no causal explanatory power. To the extent that you make
the function and the information specific, they exist only relative to observers and interpreters. Something is a thermostat
only to someone who can interpret it or use it as such. The
tree rings are information about the age of the tree only to
someone capable of interpreting them. If you strip away the
observers and interpreters then the notions become empty,
because now everything has information in it and has some
sort of "functional organization" or other. The problem is not
just that Chalmers fails to give us any reason to suppose that
the specific mechanisms by which brains cause consciousness
could be explained by "functional organization" and "information," rather he couldn't. As he uses them, these are empty
buzzwords. For all its ingenuity I am afraid his book is really
no help in the project of understanding how the brain causes
consciousness.

Chapter Seven

Israel Rosenfield, the Body Image, and the Self

So far I have been mostly discussing very general theories of consciousness. "How does the brain do it?" is the question asked by Crick, Penrose, and Edelman. Dennett denies the existence of consciousness, in the sense of subjective states of sentience and awareness, but he still seeks a general account of the brain's ability to control behavior. Chalmers tries to ground consciousness in "information," which has no special connection with the brain. In *The Strange, Familiar and Forgotten*,[1] Israel Rosenfield takes a different approach from any of the others, but one that deserves attention.

On the surface Rosenfield's book consists mostly of a series of case histories describing various forms of neural damage that people have suffered and the consequences for their mental life and consciousness. Anyone at all familiar with the standard literature of neurology, and particularly the work of Oliver Sacks, which is frequently referred to, will recognize

---

1. *The Strange, Familiar and Forgotten: An Anatomy of Consciousness* (Vintage, 1993).

some of the patients. There is the famous case of HM, who, because of the removal of the hippocampus on both sides of his brain, is incapable of preserving short-term memory. There is the case of Madame W, who, because of paralysis, cannot recognize her left hand as her own. There is the sufferer from Korsakov's syndrome whose memory came to a halt in 1945 and who in the 1980s retains the personality and memories of the young man he used to be over thirty years earlier.

However, Rosenfield wants to put forward his own view of consciousness. He is a former colleague and collaborator of Edelman, and like Edelman he emphasizes the connection between consciousness and memory. Not only is it impossible to have memory without consciousness, but equally it is impossible to have anything like a fully developed consciousness without memory. Consciousness arises from the "dynamic interrelations of the past, the present, and the body image" (p. 84). On the basis of his examination of brain-damaged patients whose reactions are disconnected and otherwise impaired, he goes on to say:

> A sense of consciousness comes precisely from the *flow* of perceptions, from the relations among them (both spatial and temporal) from the dynamic but constant relation to them as governed by one unique personal perspective sustained throughout a conscious life; this *dynamic* sense of consciousness eludes the neuroscientists' analyses. [p. 6]

In his view, it is the act of relating the moments of perception, not the moments themselves, that accounts for consciousness. The continuity of consciousness derives from the correspondence that the brain establishes from moment to moment with events in space and time. The vital ingredient in consciousness is self-awareness:

> My memory emerges from the relation between my body (more specifically my bodily sensations at any given moment) and my brain's "image" of my body (an un-conscious activity in which the brain creates a constantly changing generalized idea of the body by relating the changes in bodily sensations from moment to moment). It is this relation that creates a sense of self. [p. 8]

What is Rosenfield driving at? The best reconstruction I can make of the argument is this: when he talks about "con-sciousness," he does not mean the fact of sentience as such but rather normal, unified, non-pathological forms of human con-sciousness. Thus when he says that newborn babies are "prob-ably not conscious" (p. 60), I think he can't mean that literally. What he must mean is that they lack the sort of coherent forms of consciousness that go with memory and a sense of the self. So the book is not a theory of consciousness as such, but a theory—derived largely from studies of pathological cases—of the normal healthy consciousness of a person beyond a certain minimal age. Rosenfield's basic idea of "self-reference," which according to him is a crucial component of conscious-ness, part of the very structure of consciousness itself, in turn depends on the concept of the "body image." Neither of these notions is very well explained by Rosenfield, but they still seem to me suggestive, so I will try to clarify them.

One of the most remarkable things about the brain is its capacity to form what neurobiologists call the "body image."

To understand this, remember when I asked you to pinch your left forearm. When you did so, you felt a pain. Now, where exactly does the event of your feeling the pain occur? Common sense and our own experience tells us that it occurs in our forearm exactly in the area of the skin that we have been pinching. But in fact, that is not where it occurs. The actual event of your having a conscious sensation of pain occurs in the brain. The brain forms an image of our entire body. And when we feel pains or any other sensations in the body, the actual occurrence of the experience is in the body image in the brain.

That we experience bodily sensations in the body image is most obvious in the case of phantom limbs. In such cases, for example, a patient may continue to feel pain in his toe even after his entire leg has been amputated. It might sound as if phantom limb pains were some extremely peculiar oddity, but in fact, many of us have a version of the phantom limb in the form of sciatic pains. In the case of sciatica, the patient feels a pain in his leg, but what exactly is going on in his leg that corresponds to his pain? Exactly nothing. What happens is that the sciatic nerve in the spine is stimulated and this triggers neuron firings in his brain which give him the experience of feeling a pain in his leg even though there is nothing going on in his leg to cause the pain. The discovery of the body image is not new in neuroscience, but it is one of the most exciting discoveries in the history of the field. In a sense all of our bodily sensations are phantom body experiences, because the match between where the sensation seems to be and the actual physical body is entirely created in the brain.

It seems to me Rosenfield wants to use the body image to defend the following thesis: our sense of self is precisely a sense of experiences affecting the body image, and all experiences involve this sense of self, and hence involve the body image. This is what he calls the "self-reference" of all consciousness. All of our conscious experiences are "self-referential" in the sense that they are related to the experience of the self which is the experience of the body image. The coherence of consciousness through time and space is again related to the experience of the body by way of the body image, and without memory there is no coherent consciousness.

Rosenfield uses clinical evidence very intelligently to try to show how normal consciousness works, by contrasting it with the abnormal cases. Thus Madame I (pp. 41–45) has lost the normal body image. She cannot locate the position of her arms and legs; she is insensitive to pain and is constantly touching herself all over to try to reassure herself that she still exists. Furthermore she is incapable of normal recall of her experiences, which Rosenfield takes to support the claim that there are no memories without a sense of self (p. 41). Another example is provided by the patients with Korsakov's syndrome who cannot remember even events of a few minutes earlier. They lose all sense of time, and with that they lose a coherent sense of the self. According to Rosenfield they lack the capacity that the rest of us have to understand the ordinary meaning of words. They cannot even mean what we mean by ordinary words such as "teacup" or "clock" (p. 71).

Similarly, the patient whose arm is paralyzed refuses to recognize the limb as her own: "When her left hand was shown to her, she said, 'It's not mine, it's yours.' 'Therefore I have three hands,' the examining physician said, and Madame W answered, 'Perhaps'" (p. 57). And just as the physical trauma of paralysis creates the phenomenon of the alien limb, so great psychological trauma creates multiple personality. In such cases the great psychological pain divides the self, so that it loses an aspect of self-reference. We should not think of these cases, says Rosenfield, as matters of "inhibition" or "repression" but rather as a reorganization of the ways in which the brain responds to stimuli.

On Rosenfield's view, then, memory must not be understood as a storehouse of information, but as a continuing activity of the brain. You see this most obviously in the case of images. When I form an image of some event in my childhood, for example, I don't go into an archive and find a pre-existing image, I have to consciously form an image. A sense of self is essential to memory because all of my memories are precisely *mine*. What makes them memories is that they are part of the structure that is part of my sense of self. Memory and the self are all tied up together and are especially linked to the body image.

Rosenfield's book is not an attempt to present a well-worked-out theory of consciousness. Rather, his aim is to make some suggestions about the general nature of consciousness by studying the "deficits," or distortions, of consciousness that occur in particular pathologies. I believe the most important implication of his book for future research is that we ought to think of the experience of our own body as the central reference point of all forms of consciousness. The theoretical importance of this claim, I believe, lies in the fact that any theory of consciousness has to account for the fact that all consciousness begins with consciousness of the body. Our conscious perceptual experiences are precisely experiences of the world having an impact on our bodies, and our conscious intentional actions are typically of moving our bodies and of our bodies having an impact on the world. So from the very start, from our earliest experiences of perceiving and acting, the body is central to our consciousness. My conscious experience of my own body as an object in space and time, an experience that is in fact constructed in my brain, is the basic element that runs through all of our conscious experiences. Even when I am doing something as abstract as thinking about a mathematical problem, it is still *me* that is doing the thinking; that is, my body as this object in space and time is thinking about this problem. Not all consciousness is consciousness about the body. But all consciousness begins with the experience of the body by way of the body image.

Conclusion

How to Transform the Mystery of Consciousness into the Problem of Consciousness

1.

The enormous outpouring of letters that my original articles elicited on their publication in *The New York Review of Books* reveals that problems of the mind and consciousness are regarded with a passion that is unlike that felt for most other scientific and philosophical issues. The intensity of feeling borders on the religious and the political. It matters desperately to people what sort of solution we get to the problems that I have been discussing in this book. Oddly enough I have encountered more passion from adherents of the computational theory of the mind than from adherents of traditional religious doctrines of the soul. Some computationalists invest an almost religious intensity into their faith that our deepest problems about the mind will have a computational solution. Many people apparently believe that somehow or other, unless we are proven to be computers, something terribly important will be lost.

I am not sure I understand the source of the intensity of these feelings. Roger Penrose also remarks that when he attempted to refute the computational view of the mind his arguments were met with howls of outrage. My guess is that these strong feelings may come from the conviction of many people that computers provide the basis of a new sort of civilization—a new way of giving meaning to our lives, a new way of understanding ourselves. The computer seems to provide, at last, a way of explaining ourselves that is in accord with the scientific worldview and, perhaps most important, the computational theory of the mind expresses a certain technological will to power. If we can create minds simply by designing computer programs, we will have achieved the final technological mastery of humans over nature.

I believe that the philosophical importance of computers, as is typical with any new technology, is grossly exaggerated. The computer is a useful tool, nothing more nor less. In my own life computers have been immensely important, perhaps more important than, for example, telephones, but much less important than, for example, cars. But the idea that computers would provide us with a model for solving our deepest scientific and philosophical worries about consciousness, mind, and self seems to me out of the question, for reasons that I hope I have made sufficiently clear in the course of this book.

One of the limitations of the computational model of the mind that I have not sufficiently emphasized is how profoundly *antibiological* it is. It is a direct consequence of the definition of computation that the same computer program can be implemented on an indefinite range of different hardwares and the same hardware can implement an indefinite range of different programs. This follows from the formal (abstract, syntactical) character of computation. The result of this for the computational theory of the mind, the theory that the mind just is a computer program, in both its von Neumann and connectionist versions,[1] is that *brains don't matter.* Brains just happen to be the hardware (or wetware) medium in which our programs are implemented, but an indefinite range of other hardwares would do just as well.

I, on the other hand, want to insist that where consciousness is concerned, *brains matter crucially.* We know in fact that brain processes *cause* consciousness, and from this it follows that any other sort of system capable of causing consciousness would have to have causal powers at least equivalent to the threshold causal powers of brains to do it. An "artificial brain" might cause consciousness though it is made of some substance totally different from neurons, but whatever substance we use to build an artificial brain, the resulting structure must share with brains the causal power to get us over the threshold of consciousness. It must be able to cause what brains cause. (Compare: artificial hearts do not have to be made of muscle tissue, but whatever physical substance they are made of, the resulting structures must have causal powers at least equal to the threshold causal powers of actual hearts to pump blood.)

The computational theory of the mind denies all of this. It is committed to the view that the relation of the brain to consciousness is not a causal relation at all, but rather that consciousness simply consists of programs in the brain. And it denies that the specific neurobiology of the brain matters to consciousness in particular or the mind in general. In spite of

---

1. Von Neumann and connectionist machines and the differences between them are explained in chapter 5.

its scientific pretensions it is best to see Strong AI as a kind of last gasp of dualism. According to Strong AI the mind and consciousness are not concrete, physical, biological processes like growth, life, or digestion, but something formal and abstract. Indeed in an earlier work this is exactly how Daniel Dennett and his co-author, Douglas Hofstadter, characterized the mind. It is, they say, "an abstract sort of thing whose identity is independent of any particular physical embodiment."[2] This view expresses the residual dualism which is typical of the computationalist theory of the mind. Notice that no one would think of making a similar claim about digestion, photosynthesis, or other typical biological processes. No one would say that they are "abstract sorts of things whose identity is independent of any particular physical embodiments."

"The problem of consciousness" is the problem of explaining exactly how neurobiological processes in the brain *cause* our subjective states of awareness or sentience; how exactly these states are *realized in* the brain structures; and how exactly consciousness *functions* in the overall economy of the brain and therefore how it functions in our lives generally. If we could answer the causal questions—what causes consciousness and what does it cause—I believe the answers to the other questions would be relatively easy. That is, if we knew the whole causal story then such questions as "Where exactly are such and such conscious processes located in the brain, and why do we need them?" would fall into place. So stated, the problem of consciousness is a scientific research project

2. *The Mind's I: Fantasies and Reflections on Self and Soul* (BasicBooks, 1981), p. 15.

like any other. But the reason consciousness appears to be a "mystery" is that we don't have a clear idea of how anything in the brain *could* cause conscious states. I believe that our sense of mystery will be removed when and if we have an answer to the causal question. However, our sense of mystery is a genuine obstacle to getting an answer to the causal question. And I want to conclude the discussion of the issues raised by these six books by exploring how we might make some further progress. Let's begin by reviewing the historical situation.

Twenty years or so ago, when I first became interested seriously in these questions, most people in the neurosciences did not regard consciousness as a genuine scientific question at all. Most people simply ignored it, but if pressed, I believe they would have said that science with its objectivity could not deal with subjective states. A fairly typical attitude was expressed ironically by the University of California, San Francisco, neuroscientist Benjamin Libet, when he told me that in the neurosciences, "It is okay to be interested in consciousness, but get tenure first." Of course, not all neuroscientists have been reluctant to tackle the problem. There is a tradition going back at least to the work in the first part of the century of the great British physiologist Charles Sherrington, if not earlier, of trying to get a neurobiological account of consciousness, and this has been continued by such prominent recent scientists as Sir John Eccles and Roger Sperry. But they have been definitely regarded as mavericks in the field. Typical textbooks of brain science to this day have no chapters on consciousness and say very little to suggest that it poses an important scientific problem.

In philosophy, I believe the situation was even worse in that it was—and still is—very common to attempt to *deny* the existence of consciousness in the sense of inner qualitative subjective states of awareness or sentience. This has seldom been stated explicitly. Very few people in any era are willing to come out and say, "No human being in the history of the world has ever been conscious." But what they have offered were analyses of consciousness which tried to show that it was nothing but dispositions to behavior (behaviorism), various kinds of causal relations (functionalism), or program states of a computer system (Strong AI). The general tendency has been to suppose that consciousness could be reduced to something else, or in some other way eliminated altogether according to some version or other of "materialism."

There were complex historical reasons for the urge to deny the existence of consciousness and I have explored some of those in my book *The Rediscovery of the Mind*.[3] The simplest explanation is this: in several disciplines, but in philosophy especially, we have suffered from a pervasive fear of dualism. Many mainstream philosophers still believe that if one grants the existence and irreducibility of consciousness one is forced to accept some sort of dualistic ontology. They believe that the choice is between some version of materialism, which would deny the real existence of conscious states, and some version of dualism, which they think is implied by accepting the existence of conscious states. But dualism seems out of the question. To accept dualism is to deny the scientific worldview that we have painfully achieved over the past several centuries. To accept dualism is to conclude that we really live in two quite different worlds, a mental and a physical world, or at the very

---

3. MIT Press, 1992.

least that there are two different kinds of properties, mental and physical. I hope I have made it clear in the course of this book that I think one can accept the existence and irreducibility of consciousness as a biological phenomenon without accepting the ontology of traditional dualism, the idea that there are two metaphysically or ontologically different sorts of realms that we live in, or two different sorts of properties in the world.

What I am trying to do is to redraw the conceptual map: if you have a map on which there are only two mutually exclusive territories, the "mental" and the "physical," you have a hopeless map and you will never find your way about. In the real world, there are lots of territories—economic, political, meteorological, athletic, social, mathematical, chemical, physical, literary, artistic, etc. These are all parts of one unified world. This is an obvious point, but such is the power of our Cartesian heritage that it is very hard to grasp. In my experience, undergraduates can grasp this point fairly easily, graduate students barely, but for most professional philosophers it seems too difficult. They think my position must be either "materialism" or "property dualism." How could one be neither a materialist nor a dualist—as absurd an idea as being neither a Republican nor a Democrat!

Once we have rejected dualism, and with it rejected materialism, how should we proceed in getting a biological account of consciousness? Once we have cleared the ground of such mistakes as Strong AI and reductionism, what then? Of the books under discussion, Israel Rosenfield's does not address this question and Dennett's in effect denies the existence of the problem by denying the existence of subjective states of consciousness. David Chalmers makes the question all the more difficult to discuss by offering an account in which the brain has no special role but is only one information system among many capable of supporting consciousness. Francis Crick, Gerald Edelman, and Penrose in their quite different ways seem to me on the right track. Crick is surely right that the first step is to try to find neural correlates of consciousness. But, as I remarked earlier, neural correlates are not going to be enough. Once we know that two things are correlated, we still have not explained the correlation. Think of lightning and thunder, for example—a perfect correlation but not an explanation until we have a theory. So, what do we need after we have a correlation? Well, typically the next step in the sciences is to try to discover whether or not the correlation is a causal relation. Sometimes two phenomena can be correlated because they both have the same cause. Measles spots and high fever are correlated because they are both caused by a virus.

One way to try to figure out whether the correlates are causally related to each other is to try to manipulate one variable and see what happens to the other. So, for example, suppose we had a perfect correlation that we could observe between being conscious and being in a certain neurobiological state. I don't think, as Crick does, that it is going to be neuron firings of 40 hertz, but there will presumably be something correlated with consciousness. Let us suppose that there is some specific neurobiological state or set of states, call it "state N," which seems to be invariably correlated with being conscious. Then the next step is to find out whether or not you can induce states of consciousness by inducing state N and whether or not you can stop states of consciousness by stopping state N. If you have gone that far, then it seems to me that you have something more than a correlation, you have good evidence for a causal relation. If you can manipulate one term by manipulating the other, then other things being equal, you have very good evidence that the term you are manipulating is the cause of the term manipulated, which is its effect. This would be the first step toward getting a theoretical account. But what sort of a theory would explain how it works? What are the mechanisms supposed to be?

At this point we have to frankly confess our ignorance. Neither I nor anyone else knows right now what such a theory would look like, and I think it is going to be for the next generation of neurobiologists to provide us with such a theory. However, I am optimistic because of the following obvious and I believe decisive consideration: if we know anything about the world, we know in fact that brain processes do cause our states of consciousness. Now since we know that in fact it happens, we have to assume that it is at least in principle discoverable *how* it happens. Even if it should turn out in the long run that we do not and cannot get a causal explanation of consciousness, we cannot assume this impossibility at the start of the project. In the beginning, we have to assume that the correlations are evidence of a causal relation discoverable by us. But once we assume there is a discoverable causal relation, we also have to assume that it is theoretically explicable. It might turn out that we just cannot explain it, that the causal relation of brain and consciousness resists theoretical explanation,[4] that the problem of explaining the relation of consciousness to the brain is beyond our biologically limited

4. This is the position held by Colin McGinn, *The Problem of Consciousness: Essays Toward a Resolution* (Blackwell, 1991).

cognitive capacities, which after all were developed for hunter-gatherer environments, and not for this sort of problem. Nonetheless, we still have to assume that it is not only discoverable, but theoretically intelligible.

The dirty secret of contemporary neuroscience is not mentioned in these books and is one I have not yet discussed. So far we do not have a unifying theoretical principle of neuroscience. In the way that we have an atomic theory of matter, a germ theory of disease, a genetic theory of inheritance, a tectonic plate theory of geology, a natural selection theory of evolution, a blood-pumping theory of the heart, and even a contraction theory of muscles, we do not in that sense have a theory of how the brain works. We know a lot of facts about what actually goes on in the brain, but we do not yet have a unifying theoretical account of how what goes on at the level of the neurobiology enables the brain to do what it does by way of causing, structuring, and organizing our mental life. Like the authors of the standard textbooks, I have been mostly talking as if the neuron is the basic functional unit, and perhaps that is right. But at present we do not know that it is right. Perhaps it will turn out that trying to understand the brain at the level of neurons is as hopeless as trying to understand a car engine at the level of the molecules of metal in the cylinder block. It might turn out that the functioning causal mechanisms require lots of neurons, as is suggested by Edelman's explanations at the level of neuronal maps, or perhaps the explanatory units are much smaller than neurons, as is suggested by Penrose's discussion of microtubules. This is a factual question to be settled by further research.

But how are we supposed to get on with the research? A promising line of attack is to approach consciousness by way of the unconscious. There are plenty of clinical cases of processes in the brain that are psychologically real but which have no conscious manifestation. Perhaps the best known of these is "blindsight."[5] In these cases, the brain-injured patient is able to report events occurring in his visual field but he has no conscious awareness of the events. The patient has both eyes intact but has damage to the visual cortex at the back of the brain that makes him blind in one portion of his visual field. In a classic study the patient, DB, is blind in the lower left quadrant. If you think of the visual field as roughly resembling a circle in front of your eyes, then DB can see the right half of the circle and the top part of the left half, but he sees nothing in the lower part of the left half. In one experiment DB's eyes were focused on the center of a screen and Xs and Os were flashed on a screen exposed to the blind portion too quickly for him to move his eyes. He is asked to "guess" what was flashed on the screen. He insists that he can't see anything there, but he guesses right nearly all the time. Such patients typically are surprised at their successes. "Did you know how well you had done?" asked the experimenter in an interview after one experiment. DB answered. "No, I didn't because I couldn't see anything. I couldn't see a darn thing" (p. 24).

These experiments are interesting from several points of view but as an approach to the problem of consciousness they provide us with a way of posing the question: since the patient

---

5. See Lawrence Weiskrantz, *Blindsight: A Case Study and Implications* (Oxford University Press, 1986).

is getting something very much like the same information in both the conscious sight and the blindsight cases, what exactly is the difference, neurologically speaking, between blindsight and conscious sight? What is added by the system when the same information is apprehended in a conscious form? How does consciousness get into vision?

This is an ongoing line of research[6] and it is as promising as any I know of for cracking the problem of consciousness. If we knew how consciousness got into vision, we might then be able to locate the specific mechanisms by which the brain causes consciousness, both for vision and for other forms of consciousness. The mistakes to avoid are the usual ones that have been made over and over. We must not get sidetracked into thinking that our object of study is some third-person "objective" phenomenon, such as the patient's power of discrimination. We must not get sidetracked into thinking that we can ignore the problem of "qualia" and just study behavior, and we must not get sidetracked into thinking that there are really two kinds of consciousness, an information-processing consciousness that is amenable to scientific investigation and a phenomenal, what-it-subjectively-feels-like form of consciousness that will forever remain mysterious. No, the unity of consciousness guarantees that for each of us all the variety of the forms of our conscious life are unified into a single conscious field. This includes bodily sensations such as pains in the knee or the taste of honey; it includes visual perceptions such as seeing a rose; and it also includes thinking about

6. See P. Stoerig and A. Cowey, "Blindsight and Conscious Vision," *Brain*, 1992, pp. 147–156.

mathematical problems or the next election. Is there something it is like, or feels like, just to sit and consciously think that 2 + 3 = 5? And if so how does that differ from what it feels like to sit and think that the Democrats will win the next election? There is indeed something that it is like, or feels like, to think these things, and the difference between them is precisely the difference between consciously thinking "2 + 3 = 5" and consciously thinking, "The Democrats will win the next election."

The mystery of consciousness will gradually be removed when we solve the biological problem of consciousness. The mystery is not a metaphysical obstacle to ever understanding how the brain works; rather the sense of mystery derives from the fact that at present we not only do not know how it works, but we do not even have a clear idea of how the brain *could* work to cause consciousness. We do not understand how such a thing is even possible. But we have been in similar situations before. A hundred years ago it seemed a mystery that mere matter could be *alive*. And debates raged between mechanists who sought a mechanical, chemical explanation of life and vitalists who thought any such explanation was impossible, who thought that any explanation required us to postulate a "vital force," an "elan vital" that stood outside of mere chemical processes and made life possible. Today it is hard for us even to recover the sense of difficulty our great-grandparents' generation experienced over this issue. The mystery was resolved not just because the mechanists won and the vitalists lost the debate, but because we got a much richer conception of the mechanisms involved. Similarly with the brain. The sense of mystery will be removed when we understand the biology of consciousness with the same depth of understanding that we now understand the biology of life.

2.

I believe the best way to conclude this book is to consider the questions that keep coming up over and over in the debates and correspondence about these issues, and to put forward answers to them. Let's start with the most common question of all:

   1. Could a machine be conscious?

   We have known the answer to this question for a century. The brain is a machine. *It is a conscious machine.* The brain is a biological machine just as much as the heart and the liver. So of course some machines can think and be conscious. Your brain and mine, for example.

   2. Yes, but how about an artificial machine, a machine in the sense in which cars and computers are machines, the sort of thing you make in a factory? Could that be conscious?

   Notice that you don't ask this question about hearts. We already make artificial hearts in factories. Why should it be any different for brains? There is no more a *logical* obstacle to an artificial brain than there is to an artificial heart. The difficulties are of course enormous, but they are practical and scientific, not logical or philosophical difficulties. Because we do not know how real brains do it, we are in a poor position to fabricate an artificial brain that could cause consciousness. The essential point is one I made earlier. Because brains do it causally, that is, their inner processes actually cause them to be in conscious states, any other system would have to have causal powers at least equivalent to the threshold causal powers of the brain to do it. I intend this claim as a trivial logical consequence of the fact that brains do it causally, and I have to say "threshold causal powers" because perhaps brains have lots more than enough. In such a situation, another system would not have to have *all* the powers that brains have but it would at least have to be able to get over the threshold from nonconsciousness to consciousness. But because we are ignorant of the specific causal elements of the brain that do it, we don't know how to start making a conscious machine. Perhaps it is a biochemical feature of the neuronal structures. Perhaps it is a combination of the firing rate of the neurons and the specific neuronal architecture, as suggested by Crick. Perhaps it is the physical features of the subneuronal elements, such as the microtubules, as suggested by Penrose. Perhaps it is a feature we could duplicate in silicon or vacuum tubes. At present we just do not know. But the difficulties, to repeat, are matters of ignorance, not of metaphysical or logical obstacles.

3. But I thought your view was that brain tissue is necessary *for consciousness.*

No, that has never been my view. Rather, I point out that some brain processes are *sufficient* to cause consciousness. This is just a fact about how nature works. From this it follows trivially that any other system that did it causally would have to have at least the equivalent threshold causal powers. But this may or may not require neural tissue. We just do not know. The interest of this consequence is that it excludes, for example, formal computer programs, because they have no causal powers in addition to those of the implementing medium.

4. But then why not start by building a machine that could produce the same external effects as consciousness? If we could build a computer-guided robot that behaved as if it were conscious we would presumably have created consciousness. Why not?

As we have seen over and over in the course of this book, the essence of consciousness is that it consists in inner qualitative, subjective mental processes. You don't guarantee the duplication of those processes by duplicating the observable external behavioral effects of those processes. It would be like trying to duplicate the inner mechanisms of your watch by building an hourglass. The hourglass might keep time as well as your watch but its external behavior is irrelevant to understanding the internal structure of your wristwatch. To try to create consciousness by creating a machine which behaves as if it were conscious is similarly irrelevant, because the behavior *by itself* is irrelevant. Behavior is important to the study of consciousness only to the extent that we take the behavior as an expression of, as an effect of, the inner conscious processes.

To make this point absolutely clear, let us pin it down with an example. External stimuli cause us to have pains and these pains in turn cause pain behavior. Now, even with currently available technology we can build systems that emit pain behavior in response to pain stimuli. We could build a computer so that it prints out "OUCH!" every time you hit the keyboard hard enough. Would this give us any reason at all to suppose that we had created pains in the computer? None whatever. This point keeps coming up over and over in these debates so let me emphasize: *where the ontology of consciousness is concerned, external behavior is irrelevant.* At best, behavior is epistemically relevant—we can typically tell when other people are conscious by their behavior, for example—but the epistemic relevance depends on certain background assumptions. It rests on the assumptions that other people are *causally similar* to me, and that similar causes are likely to produce similar effects. If for example you hit your thumb with a hammer, then, other things being equal, you are likely to feel the sort of thing I feel and behave the sort of way I behave when I hit my thumb with a hammer. That is why I am so confident in attributing pains to you on the basis of the observation of a correlation between stimulus input and behavioral output. I am assuming that the underlying causal mechanisms are the same.

5. Well, that leads me to another question I wanted to ask. You keep talking about brain processes causing consciousness. But why the obsession with just brain processes? If neuron firings can cause consciousness then why couldn't information cause consciousness? Indeed you haven't shown what it is about neuron firings that is so special, and for all we know, it might be the information contained in the neuron firings.

"Information" does not name a real physical feature of the real world in the way that neuron firings, and for that matter consciousness, are real physical features of the world. Except for the information that is already in the mind of some conscious agent, information is relative to an observer. Remember the distinction I made in chapter 1 between features of the world that are observer-independent, such as force and mass, and those that are observer-relative, such as being a book or being money. Except for those forms of information that are parts of the thoughts of a conscious person, information is observer-relative. Information is anything that we can count or use as information. To take a textbook example, the tree rings contain information about the age of the tree. But what fact about the tree rings makes them informative? The only physical fact is that there is an exact covariance between the number of rings and the age of the tree in years. Someone who knows about the physical fact can infer the one from the other. But notice, you could just as well say that the age of the tree in years contains information about the number of rings in the tree stump. To put this point briefly, "information" in this sense does not name a real causal feature of the world on a par with tree stumps or sunshine. The tree rings and the cycle of the seasons are real features of the world that exist independently of us, but in that sense any information that exists in addition to these physical features is all relative to us. The upshot is that information could not be the general cause of consciousness, because information is not a separate causal feature of the world like gravity or electromagnetism. Information, to repeat, is anything in the world we can use as information. It is observer-relative.

6. *Well, what about complexity? You've left out complexity. After all, as Chalmers points out, the brain has "a trillion neurons," so why not a computer with a trillion connections? Why couldn't that be conscious?*

It is strictly speaking meaningless to talk about complexity in the absence of some criterion for, or way of measuring, complexity. But even assuming we had such a measure, say by counting independent elements of a system and the patterns of their arrangement, it is not at all clear that complexity by itself has any relevance whatever to the problem of consciousness. If we are just talking about complex patterns, the pattern of molecules in the ocean is vastly more complex than any pattern of neurons in my brain. Or for that matter, the pattern of molecules in my thumb is much more complex than the pattern of neurons in my brain simply because there are many more molecules than there are neurons. But, so what? It might turn out, indeed it is not implausible to suppose, that termites are conscious even though they only have about a hundred thousand neurons. What we need to understand is a specific biological process.

I believe that our constant urge to think that the problem of consciousness will be solved by appealing to the idea of mathematical complexity reveals some deeper mistakes we are making. If we think that information is the key to consciousness we are immediately confronted with the fact that thermostats and pocket calculators do "information processing" and it just seems too dumb to think that they are conscious. So, forgetting that information is observer-relative, we think the difference between us and thermostats is that our information processing is more complex. If only thermostats and calculators were more complicated they too might be conscious! But now the stupidity of the original move of supposing that information is the key is abetted by a kind of dizziness that comes over us when we ponder how complicated the brain really is. I have heard it claimed in hushed and almost reverential tones that the human brain is the most complex system in the whole world. The problem with this claim is not that it is false, but that it is meaningless. Relative to what kind of measure is the human brain more complex than the Milky Way or the Amazon jungle? Of course, a rich consciousness will require rich neuronal capacities. If, for example, humans are to be capable of seeing different colors—red, blue, green, etc.—the human brain will have to have a structure sufficiently rich to distinguish the different colors we consciously experience. But for the sheer existence of consciousness, complexity by itself is not sufficient. You would not increase the probability of consciousness in thermostats by rigging up a billion—or a trillion—thermostats in some complex order. To solve the problem of consciousness we need to understand the causal powers of a specific mechanism—the human and animal brain.

7. But all the same, aren't we actually making progress toward creating consciousness artificially in computers? Think for example of Deep Blue, the computer program that plays chess. At long last, we have a computer program that can beat the best chess player in the world. Even if we have not yet created a conscious computer, surely Deep Blue is a development of great significance for human consciousness?

As I said in chapter 3, as far as human consciousness is concerned, it is of no significance whatever. We have long had pocket calculators that can outperform any human mathematician. What relevance does that have to human consciousness? None at all. We have designed calculators in such a way that they will produce symbols that we can interpret as correct answers to the arithmetic questions that we have put in. But the calculators know nothing about numbers or addition or anything else. Similarly with Deep Blue. Deep Blue knows nothing about chess, moves, or anything else. It is a machine for manipulating meaningless symbols. The symbols are meaningless to it because everything is meaningless to it. We can interpret the symbols we put in as standing for chess positions, and the symbols the machine produces as standing for chess moves, because that is what we have designed the machine to do: print out symbols about moves in response to symbols about positions. We could equally well interpret the input as positions in a ballet, and the output as more choreography. It is all the same to the machine. The idea that somehow or other these or any other programs are the key to consciousness is a total fantasy.

Even more bizarre than the claim that chess-playing computers must be conscious is the claim that the existence of a program that can beat any chess master might be a threat to human dignity. To remove any temptation to this mistake, think what actually happened. A team of human researchers, using powerful electronics designed by other teams of human researchers, produced a program that will print out symbols that we can interpret as chess moves that will defeat any single human chess player. Whose dignity is supposed to be threatened by that? If the whole project of building Deep Blue had been done by chimpanzees or Martians, I might think we had some competition; but the electronic machinery has no life of its own, no autonomy. It is just a tool we have created.

8. *Well, how can you be so sure that the computer isn't conscious? It certainly behaves intelligently. Your insistence that it is not conscious looks like dogmatism. What is your proof that it is not conscious?*

You miss the point. I can't prove that this chair is not conscious. If by some miracle all chairs suddenly became conscious there is no argument that could disprove it. Similarly, I do not offer a proof that computers are not conscious. Again, if by some miracle all Macintoshes suddenly became conscious, I could not disprove the possibility. Rather, I offered a proof that computational operations by themselves, that is, formal symbol manipulations by themselves, are not sufficient to *guarantee* the presence of consciousness. The proof was that the symbol manipulations are defined in abstract syntactical terms and syntax by itself has no mental content, conscious or otherwise. Furthermore, the abstract symbols have no causal powers to cause consciousness because they have no causal powers at all. All the causal powers are in the implementing medium. A particular medium in which a program is implemented, my brain for example, might independently have causal powers to cause consciousness. But the operation of the program has to be defined totally independently of any implementing medium since the definition of the program is purely formal and thus allows implementation in any medium whatever. Any system—from men sitting on high stools with green eyeshades, to vacuum tubes, to silicon chips—that is rich enough and stable enough to carry the program can be the implementing medium. All this was shown by the Chinese Room Argument.

9. But in the end it seems to me your philosophy is just another version of materialism. All this talk about "biological naturalism" looks like old-fashioned materialism in disguise.

Materialism evolved as a way of rejecting dualism, as a way of denying that there are "mental" things or features apart from, and metaphysically different from, the rest of the "material" world. I do indeed reject dualism: but materialists also typically want to deny that consciousness is a real and irreducible part of the real world. They want to claim that it is "nothing but . . . "—and then they pick their favorite candidate to fill the blank: behavior, neurochemical states of the brain, functional states of any system, computer programs, etc. And I am denying materialism in this sense. Consciousness is a real part of the real world and it cannot be eliminated in favor of, or reduced to, something else. So I do not find the vocabulary of "materialism" and "dualism" etc. useful. I think the vocabulary creates much of our problem and does not point the way to a solution. It is possible to state the facts without using this obsolete vocabulary and that is what I have been trying to do.

10. Well, you may not like the vocabulary, but now I don't see any difference between your view and property dualism. You say consciousness is "irreducible." But what is property dualism except the view that consciousness is a property not reducible to material properties? That is, it seems your view boils down to the idea that there are two irreducibly different kinds of properties in the world, consciousness and the rest, and whatever you may want to call it, I call that view property dualism.

There are lots of real properties in the world: electro-magnetic, economic, gastronomical, aesthetic, athletic, politi-cal, geological, historical, and mathematical, to name but a few. So if my view is property dualism, it should really be called property pluralism, or property *n*-ism, where the value of *n* is left open. The really important distinction is not between the mental and the physical, mind and body, but between those real features of the world that exist independently of observers—features such as force, mass, and gravitational attraction—and those features that are dependent on observers—such as money, property, marriage, and government. Now, and this is the point, though all observer-relative properties depend on consciousness for their existence, consciousness is not itself observer-relative. Consciousness is a real and intrinsic feature of certain biological systems such as you and me.

Why then is consciousness irreducible in a way that other observer-independent properties such as liquidity and solidity are reducible? Why can't we reduce consciousness to neuronal behavior in the same way that we can reduce solidity to molecular behavior, for example? The short answer is this: consciousness has a first-person or subjective ontology and so cannot be reduced to anything that has third-person or objective ontology. If you try to reduce or eliminate one in favor of the other you leave something out. What I mean by saying that consciousness has a first-person ontology is this: biological brains have a remarkable biological capacity to produce experiences, and these experiences only exist when they are felt by some human or animal agent. You can't reduce these first-person subjective experiences to third-person phenomena for the same reason that you can't reduce third-person phenomena to subjective experiences. You can neither reduce the neuron firings to the feelings nor the feelings to the neuron firings, because in each case you would leave out the objectivity or subjectivity that is in question.

"Reduction" is actually a very confused notion and has many different meanings.[7] In one sense you *can* reduce conscious states to brain processes. All our conscious states are causally explained by brain processes, so it is possible to make a *causal* reduction of consciousness to brain processes. But the sort of reduction that materialists want, an *eliminative* reduction, one which shows that the phenomenon in question does not really exist, that it is just an illusion, cannot be performed on consciousness, for reasons I pointed out in chapter 2. Eliminative reductions require a distinction between reality and appearance. For example, the sun appears to set but the reality

---

7. For a discussion of half a dozen different senses of "reduction" see *The Rediscovery of the Mind*, chapter 5.

is that the earth rotates. But you cannot make this move for consciousness, because where consciousness is concerned the reality is the appearance. If it consciously seems to me that I am conscious, then I am conscious. And this is just another way of saying that the ontology of consciousness is subjective or first-personal.

Always ask yourself what we know about how the world works in fact. It might have turned out differently but this is in fact how it did turn out: the universe consists entirely of particles in fields of force. These particles are organized into systems. Some of these are natural systems, such as galaxies, mountains, molecules, and babies. Some are social creations such as nation-states and football teams. Among the natural systems, some are living organic systems. They contain carbon-based molecules and have heavy doses of nitrogen, oxygen, and hydrogen. On this earth they are all the result of biological evolution. Some very few of them have evolved nervous systems capable of causing and sustaining consciousness. Consciousness is caused by the behavior of microelements of nervous systems, and is realized in the structures of those nervous systems. Consciousness is not reducible in the way that other biological properties typically are, because it has a first-person ontology.

What that means is that consciousness only exists when it is experienced as such. For other features, such as growth, digestion, or photosynthesis, you can make a distinction between our experience of the feature and the feature itself. This possibility makes reduction of these other features possible. But you cannot make that reduction for consciousness without losing the point of having the concept in the first place. Consciousness and the experience of consciousness are the same thing. So we can, and indeed must, grant the irreducibility of consciousness without claiming that it is somehow metaphysically not a part of the ordinary physical world. We can, in short, accept irreducibility without accepting dualism. And accepting this reality should allow us to explore the mystery of consciousness free of the misunderstandings that have confused so many discussions of the subject.

Illustrations

Name Index

Subject Index